About the Authors

Simon Raven and Chris Raven were born in the United Kingdom. A career in overland adventure travel was launched when they drove across Siberia from the UK to Vladivostok at the dawn of a new millennium. Driving the Trans-Siberian is an account of their journey and is the second book in the 'Ravens on the Road' travel trilogy published by Samosir Books. The brothers have since driven full circle around the Black Sea, traversed the Trans-oceanic highway from the Pacific to the Atlantic coast of South America and in 2007 travelled the road to Damascus. In addition to co-writing four travel books, they have documented and photographed multiple off the beaten track destinations across the globe including China's deep south, tribal India and the Balkan peninsula. Simon and Chris have been noted by Lonely Planet for their talent to portray an "accurate view of what to expect".

Also by Chris Raven & Simon Raven

Black Sea Circuit

Carnival Express

Living the Linger

CHRIS RAVEN   SIMON RAVEN

DRIVING
the
TRANS-SIBERIAN

THE ULTIMATE ROAD TRIP ACROSS RUSSIA

samosir
BOOKS

Published by Samosir Books 2015

Copyright © Chris Raven, Simon Raven, 2015

Simon Raven and Chris Raven have asserted their rights under the Copyright, Designs and Patterns Act 1988 to be identified as the authors of this work

This book is sold subject to the condition that it shall not, by way of trade or otherwise, be lent, resold, hired out, or otherwise circulated without the publisher's prior consent in any form or binding or cover other than that in which it is published and without a similar condition including this condition being imposed on the subsequent purchaser

First published in Great Britain in 2006 by Samosir Books

ISBN 0954884272

For George

ROUTE ××××××

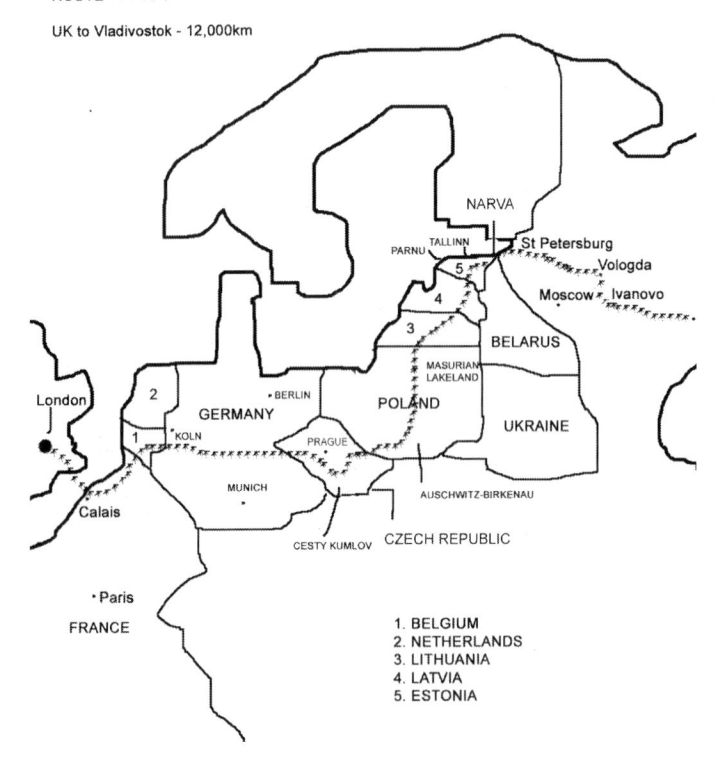

UK to Vladivostok - 12,000km

NARVA
TALLINN
PARNU
St Petersburg
Vologda
Moscow • Ivanovo
5
4
3
BELARUS
MASURIAN LAKELAND
London
2
GERMANY
• BERLIN
POLAND
UKRAINE
1
• KOLN
PRAGUE
MUNICH
AUSCHWITZ-BIRKENAU
Calais
CESTY KUMLOV
CZECH REPUBLIC

• Paris
FRANCE

1. BELGIUM
2. NETHERLANDS
3. LITHUANIA
4. LATVIA
5. ESTONIA

5hrs

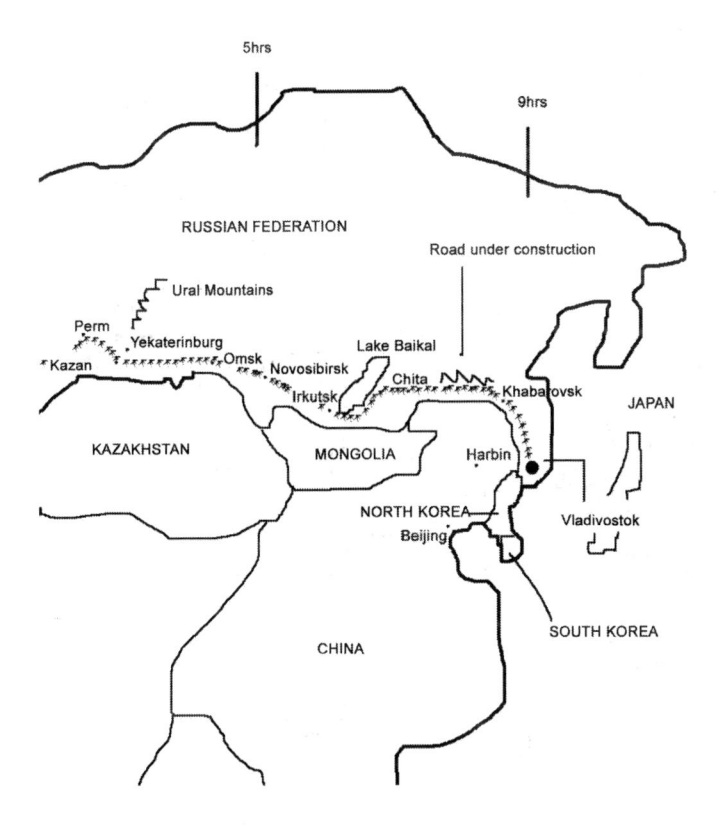

9hrs

RUSSIAN FEDERATION

Road under construction

Ural Mountains
Perm
Yekaterinburg
Kazan Omsk Novosibirsk Lake Baikal
Irkutsk Chita Khabarovsk

KAZAKHSTAN MONGOLIA JAPAN

Harbin

NORTH KOREA Vladivostok
Beijing
SOUTH KOREA

CHINA

Contents

Thirty Below
Arbeit Macht Frei
Fresh Fish
Fun Lovin' Criminals
Land of the Tsars
Coffee with the Cops
Chasing the Trans-Siberian
Bandits & Butterflies
Pearl of Siberia
Burn Baby Burn
The Final Frontier
The Amur Hellway
The Executioner
It's a Kind of Magic
Foot People
A Touch of SARS
Back to Bateman

PART 1

Thirty Below

Deep within the bow of a cross-channel ferry, passengers leap into their vehicles and watch with nervous anticipation as the bay doors slowly open like a yawning metal monster. Joining a chorus of revving engines my brother, Si, sparks up our Ford Sierra Sapphire and skids onto French soil with a satisfying clang. It's hard to beat the thrill of voyaging across the English Channel from Dover to Calais by ship. Less than five hours ago, we were crawling bumper to bumper through the congested London traffic and now we are on mainland Europe in a country famous for inventing the hot air balloon, the submarine and the parachute.

I flip open the road map. 'So we're heading north into Belgium, right?'

Si nods. 'That's correct, from Calais to Belgium, Germany to Eastern Europe, through the Baltic States into Russia, head east over the Ural Mountains, and cross the entire length of Siberia until we hit Vladivostok and the Sea of Japan.'

I slide my finger across the globe from St Petersburg to Vladivostok. The distance is immense. Siberia alone is big. In fact, if you had enormous hands you could scoop up the whole of the USA and drop it into this vast region of planet earth without even touching the sides. Add to this Alaska and all of the European countries, with the exception of Eastern Russia, and still there would be an incredible 300,000 square miles of territory left.

The idea of driving our Ford Sierra across Russia materialised late one night whilst stacking boxes of frozen oven chips in a -30°C freezer. We'd bought the car for £300 from a used car dealer and, even though it had over 100,000 miles on the clock, Si's suggestion that we attempt to drive the 1.8 litre mean machine halfway around the world seemed all too irresistible. Initially, our family and friends had thought we had finally lost the plot when we told them about our idea of driving to Vladivostok. They felt we were taking this new lifestyle of ours a little too far. Maybe we were getting a bit carried away. Six months ago we had driven a van across backcountry USA, but this didn't really give us the right to worry everyone or give us the confidence to play fools and take on the world with this massive overland adventure. A few weeks before our departure I jumped online to find out what we were letting ourselves in for. The route appeared to be impassable, with a 640km section of the proposed Amur highway, crossing the Zilov Gap between the cities of Chita and Khabarovsk in Eastern Siberia, still under construction. The completion date for this massive project linking Europe with Asia had been set for around 2010, with it fully asphalt by 2016, but it was only the summer of 2003. What chance did we have if the highway was still being bulldozed and how would we be able to make it across Siberia without a 4x4? I mentioned this to Si in passing, but he just shrugged his shoulders and told me not to worry. Deep down, I knew that if we were going to attempt this journey we might as well take the bull by the horns and go in blind.

Sandwiched between a convoy of trucks, Si speeds across the Flemish countryside at sunset. Muscular beef cattle, known as Belgian Blue, pose for the passing traffic. Crossing the invisible border into Germany we cruise on the autobahns late into the night. I feel wide-awake, which isn't surprising really as I'm still in nightshift mode. When you work the nightshift you live like a vampire. It was new to us and in a weird kind of way I soon began to enjoy my life living in the dark. Returning home at the crack of dawn after a hard night in the freezer and waking up as the sun was setting seemed totally crazy. You'd clock-in at the start of the shift feeling fit and healthy, and by the time you clocked-out you'd practically be in a wheelchair and sucking through a straw. Nobody worked in the freezer by choice, we had all ended up there through circumstance; a divorce, left the army, business collapsed. Our fellow workers were from every country imaginable, predominantly Kurdish guys from northern Iraq, but also from other places around the world such as Mozambique, Nigeria, Ghana, Congo, Serbia, Romania, Afghanistan, Pakistan, Germany, Turkey, Portugal, France, Albania and Syria to name but a few. This made working in the freezer even more fascinating, and we would spend much of the night jumping between chutes and chatting to people from all over the world. It felt like travelling, and it turned out to be as much an education as it was hard graft. One guy I got to know was called Abdul, a forty-year old man who was born in Afghanistan during the Taliban regime. He told me about the public floggings he'd received for not having a beard that was two fists in length. As a university student in Kabul, he had grown tired and fearful of the repression, and in a bid to start a new life he had fled across the border to Pakistan. He learnt Urdu and lived in Pakistan for a number of years, smuggling immigrants by camel across the border into Iran. He eventually moved to Iran himself and lived there during the entire bloody revolution and the Iraq-Iran war. After spending some time in Kazakhstan, where he taught himself to speak Russian, he travelled across Europe and eventually made it to Great Britain as an asylum seeker. He had spent the past three years trying to make a living as a tailor. The majority of the money Abdul earned in the freezer he sent back to his family in Tehran. He hadn't seen his family for over four years and had yet to meet his youngest son. We heard many stories like this during our time in the freezer, such as the guy from Mozambique whose best friend had been eaten by a huge crocodile and the guy from the Northwest frontier of Pakistan who blew up a stray dog with a rocket launcher. If this wasn't intriguing enough, the Iraq war kicked off in the last month we were working there. It was fascinating to be surrounded by the people whose country was being invaded, and to see their mixed reactions when the US army captured Saddam Hussein. Most of the Kurds were from Mosel or Kirkuk and some were from Turkey. A few of them told me how they hid under trucks, and one guy claimed he had been involved with the mafia and used to hijack cars in Baghdad.

It was around 2:30am whilst stacking boxes of frozen oven chips, when Si ran up to me with a big smile across his face and a plan that was to change everything.

'Put down that box and listen to this!' he yelled over the noise of a nearby hydraulic machine.

'Can't it wait? I've got to clear this chute before Bateman comes back.'

'Forget, Bateman. How about we drive the Ford Sierra to Vladivostok?' he beamed with excitement.

Throwing a box of oven chips into a cage, I patted my gloves together and tried to comprehend what Si was saying. 'You're joking, right?'

Si dropped his smile. 'No, I'm being deadly serious. Think about it, what a journey, driving all the way from England to Vladivostok overland across Russia and Siberia.'

'You do know where Vladivostok is, don't you?'

'Yes, of course.'

'It's near Japan.'

'Technically speaking, Chris, it's closer to North Korea.'

A voice suddenly cried out from across the freezer. 'Ravens!'

We turned to see Bateman, the evil nightshift manager, storming towards us. He was a large man who permanently wore an Aston Villa bobble hat on his head.

'What part of work don't you understand?' he growled with the manner of an army sergeant. 'What part?'

I leaned against the chute, and smiled. 'We're just warming ourselves up.'

'Look, guys, if you want to chat do it in your break. We've still got fifty thousand cases left to pick tonight. If I catch you both gossiping again like two old washer women over the garden fence you're out of here.'

Bateman stormed off and disappeared behind a chute rammed with boxes.

I turned to Si with a huge smile. 'Vladivostok. It's a crazy idea, but I love it.'

'Excellent, so in six weeks we go. In six weeks we drive the Trans-Siberian!'

Arbeit Macht Frei

It's raining heavily as we approach the Czech border. A stern-faced border official wearing a long green raincoat, steps out of his guard box and peers through the passenger window. Rainwater drips rapidly from the brim of his cap. Chris hands the guy our passports and car documents. Spinning on his heels, the official disappears into the guard box. He stamps our passports before marching back over to the car. With a nod he hands back our wet documents and waves us through. We enter the forests of Sumava and a bright bolt of lightning forks dramatically across the dark menacing sky; it's followed closely by a bone-shattering boom of thunder. The window wipers dance urgently from side to side as the clouds unleash an attack of hailstones the size of marbles. The noise is deafening and a second lightning strike illuminates our frightened faces. Visibility is zero, so we're forced to park up and wait for the storm to pass.

At sunrise, we wake up on top of a hill overlooking the Czech landscape. Deep puddles line the muddy road and the air smells sweet and fresh. After a very basic breakfast of plain crackers and a swig from a bottle of water, Chris adjusts his seat, scratches his head and starts driving. Cutting across the lush green countryside, we pass through numerous small villages and picturesque historic towns frozen in time. Spotting a photo opportunity, Chris grabs his camera and snaps a shot of a white stork feeding its chicks in a nest perched precariously on the top of a tall red brick chimney. We eventually join the highway and hurtle towards Prague. It doesn't take long to reach the city limits, and we drive across an impressive stone bridge that arches low over the Vltava River. Miraculously, Prague was completely untouched by World War II, and we're immediately wowed by the city's striking bohemian architecture. Battling through the busy, tram-infested streets, we eventually arrive outside a rather rundown hotel that is a stone's throw from the railway station. Parking beneath a concrete flyover, we check in and walk along a dark corridor to a small, musty cell like room. Collapsing onto our lumpy single beds, I stare up at the nicotine stained ceiling. The room is dark and cold with steel bars at the window. I reach over and turn on the lamp. The bulb flickers a few times before producing a dim orange glow. Fishing a towel out of my rucksack, I make my way to the communal bathroom. As I push open the door, I'm surprised to hear a guy singing 'The Lady in Red' by Chris de Burgh. Steam fills the room. Throwing my towel over the door to a vacant shower cubicle, I step inside and begin to undress.

'The-lady-in-red,' the guy shrieks, 'is dancing with meeee, cheek-to-cheek.'

Smiling at this guy's awful singing voice, I turn on the shower and quickly begin to apply shampoo to my greasy hair. The water is surprisingly hot and powerful, it lifts my mood and I have to resist the desire to join in with the rest of the chorus. After applying soap to my body, I stand with my hands by my sides and relax for a moment beneath the warm blanket of water. Feeling revitalised, I walk over to a row of large sinks and brush my teeth. A skinny middle-aged guy wearing glasses appears next to me and also begins to brush his teeth. He continues to hum, 'The Lady in Red' and we both nod before spitting toothpaste simultaneously down the plug hole.

The guy places his toothbrush inside a wash bag and turns to me with a smile. 'Did you know that toothbrushes that work with a rotation oscillation action remove more plaque and reduce gum problems more effectively than manual brushes?'

I shake my head nonchalantly. 'I didn't know that.'

'Yep, I was surprised, too. I'm Cliff by the way. Where are you from?'

'Northamptonshire,' I reply.

'Ah, famous for shoes, right?'

'Yes,' I smile. 'Are you on holiday?'

'No, business sadly. How about you?'

'I'm on a road trip with my brother. We're driving to Russia.'

'Oh, wow, that sounds like a great trip! I think you guys are in the room next door to me. I have an excellent bottle of wine I bought in Dresden. Would you both care to join me for a glass?'

'Sure.'

There's a firm knock at the door. I take a peek through the spy hole and see Cliff's big head and bulging alien eyes glaring back at me.

'Anyone home?' he sings.

Swinging open the heavy door, Cliff steps into the room clutching a bottle of wine. With his hair neatly combed to one side, he is wearing a pair of neatly pressed chinos and a white shirt.

'Goodness me,' he laughs, 'and there I was thinking my

room was shabby. Never mind, I thought I'd tempt you guys with some of the finest white wine in the world.'

'Great, I love wine,' Chris beams. 'Where's it from?'

'This little chap is from the steep slopes of the Mosel valley. Germany produces some of the lightest, most delicate white wines on the planet. You won't be disappointed.'

Whipping a corkscrew out of his pocket, Cliff extracts the cork and pours some into a glass.

'Ah, piquant and racy,' he smiles.

I sniff the contents before taking a sip.

Cliff looks at me with keen interest. 'What'd you think?'

'It's delicious.'

'Can you taste the Riesling?'

'I think so,' I reply, slightly unsure.

Shaking his head disapprovingly, Cliff pours wine into a second glass and takes a sip. He washes it around his mouth a few times before swallowing.

'Absolutely wonderful,' he smiles. 'It has that mouth-freshening enchantment that leaves your palate perky and your mind unfuddled.

I turn to Chris and smile.

'Let's get the wine flowing here,' Cliff cheerfully grins.

'Good idea,' Chris nods.

Cliff sits on a chair. 'So, what's your story, guys? Why Russia?'

'We're going to follow the Trans-Siberian railway all the way to Vladivostok,' Chris replies, sipping his wine.

Cliff's eyes light up. 'Really? Is that possible?'

'We're not entirely sure. Vladimir Putin ordered the construction of a road called the Amur Highway a few years ago, but it's not due for completion for about seven or eight years.'

'A true adventure!' Cliff laughs. 'I'd love to make a trip like that someday. I've always dreamed of travelling across Russia aboard the Trans-Siberian. If only I could. I started a new job recently working for a computer magazine. My editor offered me the opportunity to interview the chairman of a large computer company here in Prague. I jumped at the chance, although, my wife wasn't too happy. "Can't you interview him over the phone?" she said, but I kept telling her it's not how it's done. I mean, ok, we could've had a conference call, but I find it's always best to meet these fat cats face to face. Oh, and it's also a good excuse to go on a little road trip by myself. I could have flown.'

We both give an understanding nod.

Cliff leans forward. 'It's crazy how fast your life can change. Change without you even realising it.'

'How long are you going to stay in Prague?' Chris asks.

'A couple of days. There are one or two things I'd like to check out while I'm here.'

'What kind of things?'

Cliff looks uneasy. 'Oh, you know, this and that. What about you guys?'

'We'll head off tomorrow after some sightseeing. If you're interested we're thinking of crossing the Charles Bridge later and going for a drink in Stare Mesto. You're welcome to join us.'

Cliff shakes his head vehemently. 'Sorry, guys, but I'm going to have to take a rain check on that one. I'm way too tired. It's been a hell of a day. I think I'll just crawl into bed and read my book.'

* * *

Nursing killer hangovers, we check out of the hotel

around midday. Si encourages me to drive and within an hour we cross the border into Poland. We pass through a number of small grey towns and observe dozens of youths with shaved heads hanging around bus stops and drinking cans of beer at the roadside. Concrete tower blocks fill the suburbs like monuments to the soviet era. Spotting a 24-hour petrol station that serves fast food we decide to take a break. Asking a young guy inside the shop for directions to the town of Oswiecim (Auschwitz), he kindly unfolds a huge road map out on the counter and points out the route. I thank him and return to the car with a couple of giant sized hot dogs and two cups of piping hot coffee. As night falls, we find ourselves weaving through the countryside. Wisps of fog glide over the hood like spirits in the night, ghosts of the Auschwitz victims haunting our path. We eventually reach the small industrial town of Oswiecim, 40km west of Krakow. It's late and eerily quiet. We follow an old train line that leads all the way to the gates of the former Auschwitz concentration camp. Parking up outside I wrestle to get comfortable, and glance out of the window at the large brick wall that surrounds the camp. I find it impossible to remove the thought from my mind of the terrible atrocities that were carried out here during Hitler's reign of terror. In total an estimated four million Jews were killed at both Auschwitz and nearby Birkenau.

The sound of a truck's horn wakes me with a start. Vehicles of various sizes roar past on the busy main road, the swooshing of their tyres against the wet tarmac frightening us both into action. Waiting for a gap in the traffic, Si quickly swings the car out onto the road and turns into the gateway of the Auschwitz car park. We pull up beneath a giant oak tree. Taking a moment to get my head together, I open the car door and feel drops of rain on my face. I sit motionless, allowing the water to refresh my tired eyes. Scratching my head, I climb out of the car and touch my toes. My back aches and I've got a stiff neck from resting my head at a strange angle against the window. Collecting the empty crisp packets and sweet wrappers stuffed into every available orifice of the car's interior, I empty the ashtray and begin to fill a carrier bag with rubbish. Si begins to fold up all of the loose items of clothing, coats, damp socks and jumpers strewn across the back seat. Tying up the plastic bag, I walk over to a bin beneath the large oak tree and toss it inside. The lid slams shut with a satisfying clang. Feeling the heavy droplets of rainwater splashing into my hair from the branches of the tree, I take a deep breath and watch in amusement as Si struggles to change his jeans in the small confines of the car. Deciding to freshen up before heading into the museum, I rub toothpaste on my teeth and change my socks and t-shirt. In an attempt at looking smarter and possibly more studious, I dig out a shirt from the bottom of my rucksack. Switching on the radio, we listen to soothing classical music on a Polish station.

We eventually step inside the entrance to the red brick building. The foyer is eerily quiet, with black and white photographs on display of the concentration camp during WWII. A girl wipes trays behind the counter of a small cafeteria. A stern-faced woman wearing a long black raincoat and high heels marches into the building and shakes her umbrella. A tour party follows close behind and they greet us as though they are entering our home. After purchasing a ticket for the museum, everyone is ushered into a cinema. The room quickly fills with people all chaotically trying to find a seat in the dark. Hearing the projector whir into life, we watch an emotional fifteen-minute documentary about the terrible events that occurred here at Auschwitz and Birkenau. Feeling slightly traumatized we exit the cinema and are led into a courtyard. Looking around, I recognize it from the documentary and I feel the hairs on the back of my neck stand up on end. Nothing has changed. Si points out a patch of grass adjacent to the sinister barbed wire walkway, where many of the prisoners had been executed by firing squad. I shiver at the harsh reality of what took place here. Breaking away from the other tourists, we pass a tall watchtower. The spotlight glares at us like a large eye, and I get a sense of how terrifying it must have been to be imprisoned here - to live in constant fear of being shot by a bored SS guard clutching a rifle.

We approach a small grey building with a tall brick chimney, and hesitantly enter one of the main gas chambers. It was mostly women, children and the infirm that were exterminated here, those who could not work. I walk over to the window and peer out through the metal bars. We are standing in the room where new arrivals to the concentration camp had been ordered to remove their clothing. It's unimaginable to think that these poor people actually believed they were going to be given the opportunity to take a shower. I feel physically sick as I follow Si into the main chamber. Dim orange lights hang from the ceiling, and a vase of flowers has been placed in the middle of the concrete floor. I touch the damp walls and can hear the screams of the thousands of men, women and children who perished in this very room. I can see the terror in their eyes as the Zyklon B pellets, a crystallized form of hydrogen cyanide, fell around their feet from vents in the ceiling, killing them not instantly, but after fifteen to twenty painful minutes. I feel nauseous and step through an open doorway into an adjoining room. The sight of the two furnaces is too much to take in, and I find myself backing away. It's difficult to imagine how a person could physically carry out orders to extract gold teeth, collect rings, jewellery and even shave the corpse's heads before incinerating the bodies. On average 8,000 people were gassed everyday at Auschwitz and Birkenau. By the end of the Holocaust, at least four million people had been murdered, four million innocent lives taken away.

Making our way outside, the clouds burst open and the rain thunders down on Auschwitz. We run across the courtyard and take shelter beneath a doorway opposite the firing range.

'Expect to see more of what Hitler called "ethnic cleansing",' a guy shouts over in a broad Yorkshire accent.

'We've just been to the gas chamber,' I reply, shaking my head. 'It's a deeply disturbing experience.'

'That it is. I've been here before, you know. I'm a history teacher at an inner city comprehensive school in Leeds. Visiting a place like this helps me to appreciate what I teach my students. I'm here with my wife and children, Amy and Ben.'

The two young kids look wet and miserable. They peer out from the hoods of their orange raincoats.

'Say hello, kids.'

They look shyly away.

The guy's wife forces a smile, but the man either forgets or doesn't think to introduce her.

'They're all a bit tired,' he continues. 'It's been a busy few days. We flew into Warsaw on Wednesday and I hired a car. Poland is a very interesting country, but Auschwitz was on the top of my...' he turns to his wife, '...our holiday itinerary. The kids wanted to go to Spain like last year and play on the beach for the whole holiday, but I thought I'd introduce them to history instead. What better way to start than with the Auschwitz concentration camp.'

Si nods. 'Oh, I see.'

'They might not appreciate it now, but they'll benefit from this in the future.'

He turns to his wife again. She opens her mouth to say something, but misses her chance.

'When they start comprehensive school and do projects on the Holocaust, they'll be top of their class. Gold stars all round. Well, looks like the rains slowing down,' he observes, peering up at the sky. 'Come on folks, we'd better be going!'

We watch the guy march off across the courtyard, with his family trailing reluctantly behind.

Turning on his heels he calls over in our direction. 'Make sure you stop by the medical rooms. It's where they used to carry out the sterilization experiments.'

'Will do,' I wave.

We walk over to the main gates where all of the prisoners were kept. Above the gate is the sinister motto: "Arbeit Macht Frei" (work makes one free). We walk across the courtyard and pass red brick buildings where the prisoners slept. The buildings look fairly modern and are in surprisingly good condition, making the recentness of this atrocity seem even more horrifying. We pass the Death Block where prisoners who caused trouble or tried to escape died from starvation, firing squad or lethal injection. Next we examine the actual wooden beam where twelve Polish prisoners were hung, in the biggest public execution in the KL Auschwitz. Januz Pogonowski, Leon Rajzer and Tadeuz Rapacz are just three of the twelve men who died right here on this very spot. Behind glass in another block, mountains of hair, false teeth, shoes and suitcases are on display. The victim's belongings were stored in giant aircraft hangers; nothing was wasted. Even lamps were made out of skin cut from the dead. In the next block, framed photographs of people who were imprisoned at Auschwitz are hung on the wall in a long line on both sides off the corridor. I'm shocked by how similar they look to people I have known. The pictures are so clear and sharp they could have been taken yesterday. I stare into their eyes and they stare back blankly at the camera in their stripy prison uniforms. Under each photograph there is a date of how long they lasted at the labour camp. Some died after two years, some after only two weeks.

We leave Auschwitz and drive three kilometres to the vast Birkenau camp; a sub-camp of Auschwitz where the largest number of prisoners had been exterminated. With four gas chambers and three hundred prison barracks, the camp could facilitate in total up to two hundred thousand inmates. When the trains arrived, the prisoners were separated into two lines and endured what was known as the selection process. The chosen ones went to work, while the others were sent immediately to the gas chambers at the end of the line. We look around the appallingly cramped conditions of the barracks where the prisoners lived, and weave between bunk beds and stand at cracked washbasins. Returning to the main gates along the train track, I look over my shoulder at the camp one last time. I had never had much faith in humanity; Auschwitz and Birkenau only confirm this to me. As a species, we have a long way to travel along the evolutionary chain before reaching anything close to what we Homo sapiens might consider perfection.

Fresh Fish

Chris sucks the vitamin C out of a big juicy orange as we head north to the Great Masurian Lakes. Canoeists, cyclists and fishermen join us on the road and we pass large farmhouses with 4x4's parked outside. Wooden churches and windmills are dotted across the pretty landscape and canals and lakes shimmer in the distance. Driving cautiously over an old disused railway track, I can see the sparkling blue water of Lake Wigry flashing behind the trees. Pulling off the road, we crawl down a bumpy path leading to the water's edge and ditch the Sierra close to a wooden pier that reaches out across the flat surface of the lake. Walking cautiously over the wooden slats, I squat down at the end of the platform and glance out across the tranquil view. A large Canada goose hiding in the dry reeds beats its wings and lifts itself a few feet into the air, before crashing back into the water.

Rummaging through our equipment in the trunk of the car, I retrieve a telescopic fishing rod; a revolution in fishing equipment introduced sometime during the 1980s. I find some spare hooks and more line, and join Chris who has been busy digging up worms by the water's edge. Finding a suitable spot at the far end of the pier, I thread a juicy worm onto the end of the hook and make a float from a discarded ice lolly stick. Weighing the bait down by tying a stone to the line a few inches above it, I remove the spare reel from the plastic bag and attach a hook to the end. Following the same procedure I make another float, this time from a piece of bark that I manage to peel from one of the wooden planks used to make the jetty. I toss the stumpy rod over my head and catapult the bait a good six metres away. Watching the ice lolly stick bob up and down on the surface of the water, I feel instantly relaxed. Glancing over at Chris, I watch as he swings his hook backwards and forwards like a pendulum and, gathering enough momentum, he lets go of the line and casts it rather unsuccessfully into the lake. I lean back against a wooden post and smile. Like Huckleberry Finn and Tom Sawyer, minus the straw hats and dungarees, we bask in the sunshine at opposite ends of the jetty. Resigning myself to the fact that it's unlikely we'll catch anything, particularly as neither of us had managed to in our lives before, I close my eyes and enjoy the soothing sounds of the wilderness.

Being on the road is a feeling that's hard to beat. With each mile we drive I can feel the stress and worry of daily life dissolving into insignificance. For the duration of our journey, there is only the promise of new horizons and the alluring possibility of adventure. Less than a year ago, the thought of living an alternative life hadn't occurred to me as an option. I left the Midlands at the age of eighteen and moved to London. Soon after graduating from university I met a girl, fell in love and embarked on a career working as an online news editor. Life was good for a time; I had my own apartment in Shepherd's Bush, money to burn in a cool city and fantastic friends. Everything appeared to be on course and, although I wasn't completely satisfied with the mundane world of the nine to five, I hadn't considered that there might be an alternative. It had taken the break up of my relationship with Emily for me to question my future. Work no longer seemed to have a purpose. My whole game plan had evolved around earning money to support a lifestyle that may lead to marriage and children, and maybe even present me with the opportunity to buy my own home. It was what everyone around me was doing and it seemed like the most obvious path. Growing increasingly disillusioned with life in the big city, Chris's suggestion that we pack up and hit the open road sounded like an attractive possibility. Quitting my job and apartment, we bought an old van in Seattle and headed off on a road trip across America. It turned out to be one of the most frightening and yet inspiring decisions of my life so far. Our rather clumsy journey exploring backcountry USA had opened our eyes to a world outside London.

Returning to the UK after three months on the road, we found ourselves back in the hometown where we had been raised. Reluctant to return to the big city, we found temporary work in a frozen food storage facility with the idea of buying ourselves some thinking time and try and work out what our next move would be. Chris had studied photography at collage and struggled with the idea of committing to a career. He had an unquenchable thirst for adventure and was keen to stay on the move. Inspired by his enthusiasm to live a life less ordinary, I had seized hold of his coattails and was fully committed to embark on a journey of a lifetime.

During our time living in the Midlands and working in the freezer, I arranged one weekend to meet my ex-girlfriend Emily in London. We had stayed in contact for the remainder of my trip across America, and feeling confident that I could handle seeing her again after our painful break up, I jumped aboard a train and headed for the big smoke. Before I knew it, I was on Hampstead High Street for the first time since the day our relationship ended. Memories of our time together flooded into my mind and I suddenly felt anxious as to how I might feel about seeing her again. Having arrived early, I ducked into a nearby pub to calm my nerves before meeting her. Occupying a stool at the bar, I nursed a pint and enjoyed the sensation of being alone with my thoughts. Mellowed by the alcohol, I made my way to the restaurant where we had agreed to meet. Standing on the pavement, I waited patiently for her outside. Watching the traffic pass by, I tried to guess which direction she might appear from and, turning in the direction of the underground station, my heart skipped a beat when I saw her walking towards me with her big familiar smile.

'Simon!' she giggled, kissing me on the cheek.

Leaning back, she looked at me anxiously with wide eyes. 'Hey!' she laughed. 'Have you been drinking?'

'Just a pint,' I grinned. 'I got to Hampstead a bit early.'

'You piss head.'

'Come on, let's go inside.'

Taking her arm, we entered the restaurant and sat at a table by the window. Emily removed her coat and the long red scarf that I had bought for her 21st birthday. She looked as beautiful as ever, with her long shiny brown hair and clear skin. Forcing myself to avoid admiring her familiar curves, I signalled to the waiter for the menu.

'So when did you get back from America?' she smiled. 'What was it like? I want to know everything!'

'It's been a few weeks now.'

'Was it amazing?'

'It was insane!'

'I'm so jealous. You look fantastic.'

'You're looking pretty good yourself.'

Reaching across the table we held each other's hand. I knew this was a bad idea, but after four years together it just felt natural. We hadn't seen each other for nearly six months. We missed each other's company and, finding ourselves in bed together later that afternoon, I'd put the consequences to the back of my mind and enjoyed the moment. Lying in bed next to Emily, I stared up at the ceiling. I felt incredibly happy, but simultaneously an agonising sadness lay twisting in my guts. Finally, I knew it was over. I had needed to know that what I'd felt for her was something real, and feeling it more strongly than ever before I could also see that it could never work. We had grown apart. We wanted very different things, and in the pursuit of lasting happiness for ourselves we both realized it was over. In the back of my mind, I'd hoped maybe we could find something that might hold us together, but embracing her before I left her apartment that day, I knew I would never see her again and I think she knew the same.

Strolling through the streets of North London towards Camden Town, I remember feeling an overwhelming sensation of freedom. My life had changed direction for good and, despite feeling nervous about the future, I'd felt as equally excited about the endless possibilities that lay in front of me. What I did with my life now was in my hands and my hands alone. I had no one to blame for my frustrations. I could no longer use Emily or my career as an excuse not to pursue my dreams. For the first time in my life I was responsible for my destiny.

Waking up on my old friend Dermot's sofa with a killer hangover, I decided to grab something to eat from the Organic Café around the corner. Stepping into a blustery winter's day, I wrapped my scarf tightly around my neck and half-ran half-walked along the Salisbury Road.

Making myself comfortable inside the busy café, I ordered Eggs Benedict from the menu and a large cappuccino. Reading a travel article about Colombian coffee, I suddenly noticed a guy push open the door leading to the street – it was none other than my ex-boss Lawrence Cox. This was a man who had made the early years of my career a complete misery.

'Simon!' he grinned, looking surprised.

'Lawrence!' I beamed, trying to look even more surprised.

'How are you?'

'Great thanks.'

I stood up and we shook hands.

'Mind if I join you?'

'Of course not.'

Lawrence grabbed a chair and swung it over to my table. He ordered his breakfast from a passing waitress.

'So, you've returned from your travels I see.'

'I got back a couple of months ago.'

'Fantastic. How was it?'

'Incredible. It was a real adventure.'

'You went to the States, didn't you?'

'Yes, I drove from Seattle to California through backcountry America and then travelled south into Mexico.'

'Oh, how wonderful,' Lawrence sighs. 'I've always wanted to go to Acapulco and see the cliff diving.'

'I didn't make it to the Pacific Coast, but Mexico City and the Yucatan is incredible. How's Global?'

'Fabulous,' he sings, springing up in his chair. 'We've just finished a complete redesign. It looks fantastic! A lot has changed since you left. I've been promoted, actually. I'm now the Production Manager, overseeing the development of all new content. Big step, but I'm enjoying the challenge.'

'Congratulations.'

'Thanks. What are your plans now you're back?'

'I was thinking…'

'We'd love to offer you a position at Global,' Lawrence interrupted. 'But I'm afriad there isn't the head count right now.'

Stunned by his assumption, I tried to remain as calm as possible.

'But I have no intention of returning,' I reply.

Lawrence dropped his smile. 'Oh, I just thought…where are you working now?'

I hesitated before answering. 'I'm working in the Midlands at the moment.'

He frowned. 'The Midlands? What on earth are you doing there?'

'I'm working in distribution.'

'Distributing internet software?'

'No, frozen food.'

Lawrence burst out laughing. 'Frozen food?'

'Yes, I'm working in a freezer storage facility distributing frozen oven chips and pizza to the nation.'

Lawrence raised his eyebrows and snorted in my direction. 'Golly gosh, that's quite a change from Global.'

'You could say that.'

'Surely you want to move back to London.'

'I'm happy in the Midlands, thanks.'

'Where are you based?'

'Daventry.'

'Don't know it. Got an apartment?'

'No, my brother and I are crashing with our mum and her partner at the moment.'

This is almost too much for Lawrence. He burst out laughing and slammed his fist on the table. 'Oh dear,

Simon,' he beamed, wiping a tear from the corner of his eye. 'I haven't laughed like that for ages. I don't mean to be rude, but it must be hard sliding down the career ladder like that. You're certainly putting on a brave face. I wish there was something I could do to help you.'

I felt my blood reach boiling point. He had pushed me too far this time. Without warning I exploded in a torrent of rage.

'Listen here, you cock sucker!' I yelled. 'I wouldn't waste another minute of my life working for you, even if you paid me a million pounds a year and lent me your whore wife to fuck over my desk all day. You might consider behaving like an arrogant prick is an acceptable existence, but believe me, buddy, there's a whole world out there that's passing you by.'

The waitress placed Lawrence's food on the table. Jumping to my feet, I snatched a sausage off his plate and took a large bite. He looked up at me in stunned silence.

'So long, Cox.'

Storming out of the café, I could feel the adrenaline pulsing through my veins. The next chapter of my life had definitely started and there would be no turning back now.

Disturbed by a splashing sound, I open my eyes and see bubbles on the surface of the water.

'You've caught one!' Chris shouts.

Leaning over the side of the jetty, I grab hold of the line and give it a firm tug. I slowly reel it in and I can feel the weight of the fish on the end of the line. Lifting it out of the water, Chris wrestles to remove the hook from its mouth and slips it into a plastic carrier bag. Deep green in colour, the fish lies motionless on its side and gasps for air. Without warning it leaps out of the bag and onto the pier.

I dive on top of it, but the fish slips through my and flips over the side. It disappears into the lake satisfying plop. Frustrated, I squash a fresh worm onto the end of my hook. I lower it into the water and, just as I'm about to reel in the line a little, another fish leaps out of the water and takes hold of the bait.

'I've got another one!' I yell, swinging the silver fish through the air.

'Me too,' Chris hollers.

The excitement of catching a fish is overwhelming and, despite struggling with the guilt of killing a living creature, we quickly get used to the idea; particularly the hungrier we become. Returning to the car with our catch, we feel like proud hunters returning to the village with a feast. I immediately grab the SAS Survival Guide.

'What does it say about gutting fish?' Chris grins, pouring a drop of oil into the frying pan.

Thumbing through the pages, I find the "Fish and Fishing" section. 'It says here that all freshwater fish are edible. Those fewer than five centimetres in length need no preparation and larger fish must be gutted.'

Following the guidelines in the book, we scrape off the scales, gut one or two of the larger fish and place them into the hot pan. They sizzle and curl up in the heat. I pick off a piece of flesh and pop it into my mouth. It tastes delicious. After a hearty meal and a beer, I feel satisfied that although our culinary skills may need some improvement, tonight at least we have proven to ourselves that we can survive in the wild.

Fun Lovin' Criminals

The stench of fish is overpowering. It's up my nose, it's in my hair and I hear a low growl in my stomach and fear it's the fish taking their revenge. Si is nowhere to be seen and his sleeping bag lies unzipped on the passenger seat. I scan the area for traces of his whereabouts and smile when I see him stumble from behind a bush clutching a toilet roll.

After breakfast and a refreshing swim, we drive to the Polish border at Budzisko and cross with ease to the Lithuanian town of Kalvarija. We continue north along a brand new stretch of highway that carries us towards the city of Kaunus. I flick through the guidebook and I'm fascinated to learn about Lithuania's recent past. In 1989, the year before the country had proclaimed independence from Russia, an astonishing two million people had created a human chain by joining hands in a peaceful protest with Latvians and Estonians. Known today as the Baltic Way, this symbolic act of resistance, united people from three different countries and stretched for 600km (about 370 miles). Lithuania was the first country to break away from the Eastern Block, which inspired other countries to follow. From out of nowhere, a horse pulling a cart cuts across the highway in front of us, forcing Si to brake sharply and swerve to the left. The smell of our burning brakes fills the air. The old guy driving this ancient mode of transport thrashes the horse's reins, while a woman wearing a headscarf clings on for dear life in the back. They fly down a steep embankment before disappearing into a field. Heading for the Baltic Sea, we turn west onto the A1 and cross the Nemunas River. Reaching the industrial city of Kaunas, we avoid the centre and hurtle past a large industrial power station that bellows thick black smoke into the air from towering red and white striped chimneys. Approaching the Latvian border, I pull up at customs control and a jolly gentleman with rosy cheeks steps out of a booth. He beams a smile and stamps our passports before gesturing for us to drive right through. We push on into the evening and head for the capital city of Riga; the largest city of the Baltic States and the host of this year's European Song Contest. The city lights twinkle in the distance, and we cross an impressive suspension bridge that carries us over the river Daugava and into the World Heritage historic centre. We wander through the pretty streets, brimming with art Nouveau and Jugendstil architecture. Riga was a centre of Viking trade during the early Middle Ages. It later became a member of the Hanseatic League in 1282, which was instrumental in giving Riga economic and political stability. During World War II, Latvia was occupied by the Soviet Union and later by Nazi Germany in 1941–1944. The city's Jewish community was forced into the Riga Ghetto and a Nazi concentration camp was constructed. The Soviet Union re-entered Latvia in 1944 and it stayed under Soviet control until the country reclaimed independence in 1991.

Returning to the wilderness once more, in a country that has a long tradition with conservation, Si narrowly avoids colliding with a large deer that leaps across the road. In the fading light, we park for the night in the tranquil setting of the Gauja National Park. At sunrise, we trek deep inside the park before continuing on our scenic journey to the northern Baltic State of Estonia. We reach the outskirts of the seaside resort of Parnu around four o'clock in the afternoon. We're welcomed by a row of billboards advertising campsites, restaurants, bars and an endless list of holiday activities. We check into a hotel in the centre of town and the incredibly tall blonde woman working behind reception, whose head is literally brushing against the ceiling, shows us to a large clean room with six single beds. It's a relief to find comfort after almost a week living on the road. Keen to celebrate our arrival at the Russian frontier, Si cracks open a bottle of red wine and we agree to treat ourselves to a night on the town.

Heading into the street feeling fresh and buzzing from the wine, we sit outside a tavern and devour a juicy steak. We chat to a friendly group of guys from Helsinki, who crossed the Baltic by ferry. They recommend we check out the Mirage nightclub and, curious to observe how the Estonian's party, we head for the club with a skip in our step. We join a long queue of people outside and fight our way to the bar. The dance floor is already crowded with an interesting mix of smiley, eccentric individuals. An attractive girl wearing a short yellow skirt grabs Si's hand and begins to dance around him. Swept away by the crowd, I'm pushed towards the edge of the dance floor.

I turn to the guy standing next to me. He's wearing a black leather jacket and has a scar across his cheek.

'All right, mate,' I smile.

'You Arab,' he grunts with a thick Russian accent.

'No,' I reply, surprised by his question.

'I from Chechnya,' he snaps, pointing proudly at his chest.

Removing a half litre bottle of vodka from his jacket pocket, he unscrews the lid and pours some into my glass.

'Nostrovia,' he winks, taking a large swig from the bottle.

I follow his lead and do the same.

I point at my chest. 'I'm Chris from England.'

'I Sergei from Grozny.'

I reach out to shake his hand, but he ignores me and takes another swig.

'You live in Parnu?' I ask trying hard to keep the conversation flowing.

'Nyet, I here five year.'

'Do you work here?'

'Nyet, I Chechen criminal,' he replies sternly.

I flash a smile. 'A Chechen criminal?'

He nods. 'Da, Chechnya no good too much guns, so I come Estonia. Why you Estonia?' he commands.

'I drove here from England with my brother. We're heading to Vladivostok.'

Sergei roars with laughter. 'You drive Vladivostok?'

'Yes, in a Ford Sierra.'

He playfully pushes me with his fist. 'You make joke.'

'It's true!'

He roars with laughter before refilling our glasses. 'Impossible. Not even Chechen soldier do this.'

'Why not?'

Sergei draws a finger across his throat. 'Too much danger, many bandits...you will die!'

A guy with olive skin wearing a black roll neck jumper slides up next to Sergei. I discover Azamat is also from the city of Grozny in Chechnya. Sergei talks to him in Russian. They both turn to me and laugh.

'You will die!' Azamat repeats, tossing his head back and roaring with laughter.

Desperate to change the subject, I interrupt the laughter and ask Azamat what he is doing in Parnu.

'I Chechen criminal,' he replies proudly.

'You as well?' I grin.

He frowns and turns to Sergei. Sergei turns to me and nods.

I clear my throat. 'Oh, uh, cool.'

Across the crowded dance floor I see Si pushing his way towards the bar, so I offer my new criminal friends a drink.

'You want vodka?' I ask, knowing that this is a stupid question.

Sergei nods. 'Da, spaceeba, Chris from England, spaceeba.'

I leap on the bar stool next to Si.

'Hey, hot shot!' he grins. 'Where did you go?'

'I got swept away by the crowd.'

'Of course you did. Just ride the music, man.'

'"Ride the music". I'm quite happy chilling out on the sidelines, thank you very much. I've been chatting to two Chechen criminals.'

'What?'

'Sergei and Azamat, they're both criminals from Grozny in Chechnya. I'm going to buy them a drink.'

'Back up there, buddy. Did you just say Chechen criminals, as in criminals from Chechnya?'

'Yep.'

'What kind of criminals?'

I shrug. 'No idea, I didn't ask, I'll ask them.'

'No, they could be dangerous. I'd stay well away from them if I were you. It can only lead to trouble.'

I stumble out of the Mirage nightclub around 3am and slide onto the wet pavement. There is a slight chill in the air and a police car with its blue flashing lights is parked up nearby. Two cops lean against the hood and look amused, as they watch a group of women tottering down the street wearing impossible high heels. I lost Sergei and his friend Azamat somewhere between going to the bar and chatting up Betty Boop, who turned out to be from the dark corners of Berlin. Si is still in the club dancing to Iggy Pop. I try to stay focused despite feeling severely inebriated. Everybody standing outside begins to either climb into a taxi or disappear on foot down the main shopping street. Not wishing to be left alone with two bored cops, I head off in search of the hotel. Staggering through the dimly lit streets, I turn left and then right in the direction of a big road, which I think, is near to where we are staying. Within seconds I'm lost. The wind starts to pick up and I scan the area for recognisable landmarks. A brightly painted church on the corner looks vaguely familiar, although, I can't be sure. Taking a few deep breaths, I try to think clearly and decide to turn around and walk back to the shopping street. The last thing I need is to end up on some crack estate on the outskirts of town. Rubbing my eyes, I try to stay focused and zigzag back through the wet streets. The buildings either side of the road are in darkness and, apart from the occasional swoosh of a car driving by or a dog barking somewhere in the distance, it's eerily quiet. I reach a crossroads and stop at the corner as I try to retrace my steps. How difficult can this be? This is ridiculous. I just walked down here a few moments ago. I notice a guy in a brown bomber jacket walking towards me. I straighten my posture and try to look as though I know where I'm going. He shouts over, but I'm unable to understand what he's saying. He crosses the road and approaches me. I stand my ground, annoyed with myself for not paying more attention to Jackie Chang's karate moves in the movie 'Rumble in the Bronx'.

'You want woman?' he grins, puffing on a cigarette.

I frown. 'Woman?'

'Da, jiggy-jiggy boom boom.'

'Nyet, thank you.'

His eyes are immediately drawn to my jacket pocket. I begin to feel uncomfortable. Distracted by a passing car, I look away for a split second and before you can say "Jackie Chang", he reaches inside my pocket and grabs a couple of notes I'd stuffed in there for safe keeping. In complete shock I watch him run off. I instinctively chase after him and shout really scary things like, "I can use a gun, you know!" and "the police are coming!" but he finds my threatening words rather amusing and laughs over his shoulder. After a hundred metres it slowly dawns on me that pursuing this guy is actually quite a bad idea. There can't have been more than ten euros in my pocket. I'm certainly not going to be knifed to death or shot in the head over such a small amount of money. I skid to a halt and watch the thief disappear out of sight. Feeling foolish and annoyed with myself for placing myself in this vulnerable situation, I pick up pace and eventually find my way back to the main shopping street. Feeling relaxed after regaining my bearings, I head purposefully in the direction of the hotel.

* * *

I wake up fully dressed and lying outstretched across three single beds. Keen to hit the road, I head downstairs and throwing our bags into the trunk of the car. Chris appears with a deep crease running down the side of his face and slumps into the passenger seat. Buying a strong coffee we drive north to Tallinn, the capital of Estonia, with soothing classical music playing on the stereo. Under the rule of German Order from the 13th-16th-Century, Tallinn was a flourishing Hanseatic trade centre. Salt was the main good that boosted the wealth of the local merchants and left a mark in Tallinn's grand architectural legacy. We park up a short distance from the Memorial to the Victims of the Estonia Ferry Disaster, which tragically claimed the lives of 852 people in 1994 when the MS Estonia sank during a scheduled crossing from Tallinn to Stockholm. Joining the hoards of summer tourists, we wander around the castle walls of this enchanting city and admire the tall church spires and restored medieval and hanseatic architecture and Art Nouveau style buildings that spring out at every turn. Chris takes my photograph in front of the impressive Alexander Nevsky Orthodox Cathedral, and we watch playful actors dressed in 14th Century costumes entertaining the crowds in the colourful Town Hall Square. Devouring a plate of rosolje, a popular Estonian dish based on beetroot, potatoes and herring, we push east along the northern Baltic coast.

In the late afternoon, we rejoin the Tallin-Narva Highway and pass through the stunning Lahemaa National Park "Land of Bays". We walk a short three kilometre trail and inhale the strong scent of pine needles and the salty sea air. This strip of coast has a stony and sandy shoreline with picturesque bogs, where alvars and rivers have cut deep groves into the limestone cliff. The pine forests are strewn with erratic boulders, some the size of a two-storey house that were carried over from Finland thousands of years ago by continental ice. Lahemaa was the first national park in Estonia and indeed anywhere in the former Soviet Union. Shipbuilding used to be popular here and centuries ago ships made of Lahemaa pine sailed the seven seas. It is also one of Europe's most important forest conservation areas and is inhabited by moose, boars, bears and lynxes. Knocking the mud from our trainers, we boil a pan of water and drink a coffee before driving the last few miles to the Russian border. We arrive in Narva at sunset, which seems incredible when you consider it's nearly eleven o'clock at night. On the forecourt of a 24-hour petrol station, we park up next to a Russian articulated lorry. Lying very still with my sleeping bag pulled over my head, I begin to feel anxious. A million images flood into my mind of Stalin and Lenin, the Cold War, the KGB, concrete tower blocks and freezing cold weather. As a child I recall watching news footage of Boris Yeltsin standing on top of a tank during the coup in 1991, and seeing the queues of people in Red Square when Russia opened its first McDonald's. From what I have read and seen on the news, Russia is a country filled with danger and mystery and, being so close to the border for the first time in my life, I begin to fear what lies ahead.

My alarm wakes me with a start. It's 4:45am and it's already starting to get light. Knocking back a strong cup of coffee, we drive through the deserted streets and follow signs to the border. Weaving through the backstreets of Narva, we eventually approach an official checkpoint. We walk over to a small control booth and proceed to have a very confusing conversation with the impatient woman inside. She waves to her colleague, who dashes over and explains to us that we need to drive to a different building to get a form. He agrees to take us there. Making space for him in the back, Chris feeds the guy sweets as he directs us to a small brick building at the far end of a car park. We queue up behind a dozen old Ladas and he leads us both to the office. The official sitting inside stamps our documents and hands me a receipt. Our personal escort chats to the official and they both turn to me and laugh. I get the distinct impression they find my long hair amusing. Returning to the previous checkpoint, our documents are stamped and we're directed to the Friendship Bridge, which stretches across the Narva River. We join a second queue of cars. I watch the sun rise over the Russian town of Ivangorod and admire two medieval castles that face each other on either side of the bridge, one in Estonia and the other in Russia. After twenty minutes, all of the car engines begin to splutter into action, and we slowly inch forward. Reaching the barrier, we're instructed to cut the engine and two officials check under the hood and rummage through the junk in the boot. Much to our relief everything appears to be to their satisfaction, and we're waved through to the next stage. Drawing alongside yet another control booth, we hand over our passports and all of the relevant documentation for the car. The stocky woman behind the counter thumps a stamp on an empty page in our passports, and then proceeds to shout something at me in Russian. Tapping her watch, she points back in the direction of Estonia. Realising she wants to know how long we will be visiting the country, I quickly scribble down a rough date. She mutters something and sends us away with a flick of her wrist. Exiting the final barrier, we crawl along a bumpy road and as if by magic we suddenly find ourselves on Russian soil.

PART 2

Land of the Tsars

Our first experience of Russian roads is a quiet country drive along a potholed stretch of tarmac that is in urgent need of repair. A white Lada appears in the rear view mirror. It seems to be quite a distance behind us, but when I look again I notice it has picked up speed and is now kissing our bumper. Si suggests we let it overtake, so I dab the brakes and it speeds right past. The young guy driving proceeds to slow down again in front of us. I begin to wonder if he is intrigued by our foreign machine with the strange license plates, or if he's just curious to see the faces of the people inside. Not wishing to disappoint I put the pedal to the metal and overtake the small boxy vehicle, but the driver of the Lada begins to speed up. Driving side by side, I'm forced to either drop down a gear and give it some power or slow down; I choose to give it some power. Impressed by the Sierra's monstrous acceleration, we zoom off into the distance. I watch with satisfaction as the Lada shrinks in the wing mirror. All of a sudden, I see a car heading towards us with its headlights flashing. The driver waves a black and white baton furiously out of the window. It's the GAI. Slamming on the brakes, I swerve to the side of the road and park up next to a goat chewing on grass. It glances over at us and then at the police vehicle pulling up behind.

Si shakes his head. 'Five minutes in Russia and already the cops have stopped us for speeding.'

A stocky police officer climbs out of the small cop car, and slowly makes his way over to the Sierra. He's incredibly short and has a bushy moustache.

'Dobraye ootra,' he mutters, peering through my open window.

'Dobraye ootra!' We sing in unison.

The officer indicates for me to step out of the vehicle. Si hands me the phrasebook and the car documents. Feeling nervous I try to look as confused as possible, which isn't all that difficult, and point at the phrasebook. The officer ignores me and studies the GB sticker and the registration plate at the back of the Sierra. Thankfully, we'd cleaned the car before entering Russia so at least he can't fine us for driving a dirty motor, which is illegal under Russian law.

'Kooda vi eedyotye?' he mutters.

Si sticks his head out of the driver's window. 'Explain to him that you don't speak Russian.'

I flick through the phrasebook. 'Ya plokha gavaryoo pa-rooskee.'

The officer pulls a map of Russia out of his jacket pocket. He shows it to me and I point to St Petersburg. He nods and asks for our passports. He studies our business visas for a brief moment before handing them back. Waving me over to the cop car, he swings open the rear passenger door and gestures for me to get in. I contort my lanky body inside the dwarf-mobile, and smile at a second officer who occupies the front passenger seat. He's much thinner in the face and is wearing thin metal-framed glasses. The officer with the scary moustache looks at me without smiling, and proceeds to flick through a series of laminated cards displaying speed limit signs. After a few seconds the driving lesson is over and, as a kind gesture, I'm asked to hand over fifty euros for driving 55mph in a built up area. Suspecting that I'm being seriously ripped off, I struggle to think of a way out of the situation without being dragged down the station. Cursing under my breath, I pull out my tatty wallet and reluctantly hand over a crisp fifty-euro note. The officers look incredibly pleased with themselves and, not hanging around to socialize, they proceed to speed off in a cloud of exhaust fumes. I jump behind the wheel.

'Fifty euros!' Si yells. 'Are you sure it wasn't fifty rubles?'

'Hey, I was under pressure. My mind was doing summersaults.'

'If this happens to us everyday we're screwed. Did you try and negotiate? Did you get a receipt?'

'I haven't just bought a pair of slacks. We've been fined.'

'But you're supposed to get a receipt.'

'Well, I didn't get one. Look, I was speeding in a built up area. They caught me red handed.'

Si looks around, and frowns. 'A built up area? What, two sheds and a goat?'

We look over at the goat and burst out laughing.

Heading back on the road, the traffic begins to increase in volume as we draw closer to St Petersburg. Wary of the speed limit we approach a GAI checkpoint. Half a dozen officers in uniform stand at the roadside swinging their batons, but much to our relief we skip by without being stopped. Rolling through the industrial suburbs of the city, concrete tower blocks and rusty railway tracks stretch out in every direction. Si takes over the driving and does well to match the aggression of his fellow road users, while I work hard at being his second pair of eyes and point out trams hurtling towards us. Pushing into the heart of the city we eventually reach Nevsky prospect, the main shopping street. We decide to stay the night at the HI St Petersburg Hostel, which is located a few streets back from Nevsky prospekt and the train station. The guidebook informs us that the staff are "preternaturally friendly", and all prices include breakfast. Chasing a Ghostbusters style ambulance, Si turns right and hurtles down a residential street. He pulls up outside the hostel. I grab the guidebook and offer to check things out. Racing inside the building, I make my presence known to the middle-aged woman behind the reception desk, who is wearing a burgundy jacket with enormous shoulder pads.

'Dobraye ootra,' I smile.

The woman glances down at her watch. 'Dobriy dyen,' she replies sternly. She sighs. 'How can I help you?'

I whip my passport out of my money belt. 'I'd like a room for two people, please.'

She doesn't respond.

'We also need to register our business visas.'

'Nyet, only tourist visas.'

'I see. Can you recommend a hotel in the area that can help us?'

She shakes her head. 'Nyet.'

I find the extent of her rudeness almost amusing. The woman turns away and begins shuffling a pile of paper on the desk. Without saying goodbye, I leave the hostel and run back to the car. Scanning through the guidebook the only place that promises to register business visas is one of the larger hotels, so we make our way to the Hotel Oktyabrskaya; a grand white building situated opposite the Moscow train station on Ligovsky prospekt. Si offers to check things out and returns ten minutes later with a skip in his step.

'We've got a room,' he smiles, looking extremely pleased.

'How much is it?'

'One hundred and fifty euros.'

'What! We can't afford that.'

'Don't panic. Think about it. If we'd stayed at the other hostel a room would've been at least fifty euros, plus another thirty to register the visas. They do it for free here. Add on another twenty for parking the car somewhere safe overnight. This is an extra fifty euros and we get to stay in luxury for once in our lives.'

Grabbing our rucksacks from the trunk, we race up the steps and shuffle through the revolving doors. The reception area is huge, with grand chandeliers hanging from the enormous decorative ceiling. Two meathead doormen watch us suspiciously as we make our way over to the enormous marble reception desk. We hand over our passports and the receptionist slides over the room key. Squeezing into the plush lift, we make our way to the second floor and find our room. It's a huge suite with a separate lounge area. We crack open a bottle of beer from the refrigerator and celebrate our arrival in the land of the Tsars.

* * *

Under strict orders from Chris to purchase beer, I march through the busy streets of St Petersburg and go in search of food. Crossing ploshchad Vosstania, I spot a large outdoor market. Small kiosks selling beer, cigarettes and fast food run down the centre of a pedestrian street. Stumbling across a stall selling whole roasted barbecued chickens, I dive inside my pockets and claim the largest bird. Happy with my purchase, I grab a large two-litre bottle of beer before returning to the hotel. Passing the Sierra, I smile at the sight of our old banger parked up outside the grand entrance to the hotel. It looks out of place next to the shiny new vehicles parked either side. Trotting up the steps I nod to the doorman, who proceeds to eyeball me all the way over to the elevator with my greasy chicken. Choosing the stairs for fear of stinking out the lift, I propel myself to the second floor and make my way down the corridor. Pressing the bell outside our room, I hear Chris fumbling with the lock. He swings open the door, and I look in surprise at him standing in the doorway in his boxer shorts covered in sweat. Following him inside, he disappears into the bathroom and I watch in amusement as he begins to wring out a t-shirt in the gigantic bathtub.

I frown. 'What the hell are you doing?'

'Washing my clothes,' he smiles.

'Use the hotel laundry service, you freak.'

'Have you seen how much they charge? It's about a dollar a sock.'

Scratching the back of his head with irritation he leaves a crest of soapsuds in his hair. Chuckling to myself, I walk from the entrance hall into the extravagant main room and place the chicken on the glass coffee table. Chris appears a few minutes later and begins draping his wet clothes around the room; hanging them from every chair, door handle and window catch in sight. He wipes the sweat from his forehead on a towel before collapsing onto the large corner sofa. Tucking into the chicken, I grab a couple of chunky glasses from the bathroom and open the large plastic bottle of beer. We make plans to "paint the town red", but switching on the TV, we stretch out on our comfortable beds and within seconds we're both fast asleep. Rock 'n' Roll!

Sunlight streams through the window. I climb out of bed like an old man and flick on the TV. It's 6:27am. I haven't slept this well for years. It almost feels quite strange to experience such comfort. Making my way into the bathroom, I pull the chunky brass lever at the end of the bathtub. Water from the large showerhead engulfs me and using the complimentary exfoliating shower gel I pour some into the palm of my hand and work up lather all over my body. Washing away the soapy grit, I feel like a snake that has just shed its skin. Dancing across the heated marble bathroom floor, I'm embraced by the warmth of an enormous bath towel. Slipping on a robe, I brush my teeth and shave my patchy stubble in the large mirror. Studying my face, I grin at the fresh-faced boy staring back at me and realise that a touch of luxury every now and then certainly rejuvenates the soul, although, the satisfaction of getting dirty first makes it all the more enjoyable.

We step into the elevator and make our way down to breakfast. Arriving in the dining hall on the ground floor, we gasp at the sight of the banquet laid out in front of us. A line of chefs wearing tall white hats, cook everything from omelettes, sausages, bacon and fried bread on command. There's an entire table dedicated to an enormous selection of cold meat and cheese and another piled high with fresh fruit, French bread, croissants, toast, five flavours of jam, honey, marmalade, cereals, tea, coffee and hot chocolate.

Chris looks at me in utter bemusement. 'Is this all for us?'

'It is indeed, fat boy. Tuck in, we need to try and get our money's worth.'

Loading up our plates with a full English breakfast, we

return for the continental. Chris piles a plate high with meat and cheese, and carefully manages to balance a couple of yogurts on top. Returning for seconds and thirds, we eat and eat and eat and even find room for more sausages and bacon before loading up our pockets with packets of biscuits and fruit. Feeling nauseous, we waddle out of the dining hall and return to the room to let our food digest. We hang around in luxury for a few more hours before checking out at eleven o'clock on the dot. The slim, assertive girl on reception hands back our passports and informs us that our business visas are now registered.

Throwing our rucksacks into the trunk, we walk along Nevsky prospect. Grand mansion buildings tower above us, and smartly dressed commuters hop on and off trams. A Russian businessman rushes past an advertising poster for L'Oréal lipstick, with his hands buried deep in his jacket pockets and a cigarette protruding from his mouth. Crossing the Fontanka Canal, we pass the Catherine the Great Statue and eventually arrive at the huge Gostiny Dvor Department Store. Nevsky prospect was once one of the grandest boulevards in the whole of Europe, and admiring a stream of colourful shops, galleries and banks we turn left and pause outside the lavish Grand Hotel Europe. Through the open doorway of the hotel, I can see a sweeping staircase and a reception filled with brightly polished antique furniture. Everything gleams. A beautiful reconditioned racing green Aston Martin is parked outside. A banner draped across the hotel's main entrance reads "The London to St Petersburg Classic Car Rally". Looking up at the elegant balcony, a group of well-dressed gentlemen in tweed chatter and laugh noisily as they smoke cigars and drink champagne above our heads.

Chris draws an invisible banner in the air. '"The Ravens on the Road Ford Sierra Rally", what do you think?'

I smile. 'Glamorous. It's crazy to think they're celebrating the end of their journey when ours has only just begun.'

Sitting on the banks of the Griboedova Canal, we admire the spectacular beauty of the multi-domed Church of the Resurrection of Jesus Christ. Also known as the Church on Spilt Blood, it was built on the exact spot where Alexander II was fatally wounded in an assassination attempt in 1881. Chris whips out his camera and takes a few shots of the gold, blue and white patterned onion domes on top of the towering Cathedral, apparently designed to imitate the romance of a candle flame. Opposite the Kazan Cathedral we check out a beautiful art nouveau building, which once housed the old Singer sewing-machine company. These days it's now home to St Petersburg's premier bookstore, Dom Knigi. It's the perfect place to buy a road atlas that covers the entire road network for Russia and Siberia. With the lure of Russia calling, we head back to the Raven mobile and make a move to the city of Vologda.

Coffee with the Cops

Si matches the aggression of our fellow road users as we battle through the rush hour traffic. Before we know it we're on the potholed M18 that carries us east out of the city. Skimming alongside the enormous Lake Ladoga we pass a turn off for Murmansk, a city eight hundred miles north of St Petersburg on the Barents Sea. At this time of year the Arctic coast of Russia experiences daylight around the clock. I munch on a bruised apple and watch an unbroken forest flash by my window for hundreds of miles.

We stop for petrol in the late evening. A truck driver wearing a blue shirt and jeans fills his vehicle with diesel. An excited kid, who I assume is the guy's son, jumps around excitedly in the driver's cab. Collapsing out of the car, I stretch my aching body. Si tears open a packet of biscuits and quickly butters some rolls. The petrol station is eerily quiet. There doesn't appear to be anyone around. I lift up the hood and check the oil and water. With limited knowledge of the workings of the internal combustion engine, I peer down at the mass of oily black pipes and an engine that looks like it has been salvaged from the bottom of the ocean. I prod a pipe next to the alternator that doesn't appear to be connected to anything. What exactly is its purpose? I suddenly experience a feeling of doubt. We are about to attempt to drive across the notorious Siberian wilderness in a sixteen year-old saloon car designed for smooth tarmac highways. Moving over to a petrol pump, we decide to grab some fuel before we head back on the road to Vologda. Grabbing the hose I feed it into the tank, but nothing happens, so I hook it back in place and walk over to the small brick building with blacked out windows. Cupping my hands I peer through the glass, but all I can see is my puzzled face looking back at me. Noticing a metal pole with a plastic handle jutting out from below the window, I take hold of it and find it's attached to a metal tray. It looks as though this might be how you pay for your petrol without having to see or speak to the person inside. You pull out the tray, put your money inside and slide it through the gap in the window. Now, if I'm not mistaken, this kind of set up is either for really antisocial petrol station attendants, who can't be bothered to deal with customers face to face, or it's to prevent bloodthirsty bandits from robbing the joint. Deciding to give it a go, I place a 500-ruble note in the metal box and slide it inside. I'm surprised to hear a woman shouting at me from behind the glass. Seconds later the metal box comes flying back out at me. Leaping to one side, the metal bar misses my groin by a few millimetres. Confused and slightly offended by the attendant's aggression, I grab my money and return to the car.

We arrive in Vologda in the late evening. It's still daylight and we pass soldiers in uniform strolling along the street with their oversized hats and long coats. We're only a day's drive from the tourist hotspots of Moscow and St Petersburg, yet already it feels like we're deep within this alien world. The city of Vologda was the playground of Ivan the Terrible and is our first introduction to the Soviet years. The Kremlin, with its silver onion domes dominates the skyline, as does the nearby golden spire of the St Sofia's Bell Tower. Following the Vologda River, we take a stroll around the statue of Lenin close to the market square. The city centre is a hive of activity with local people going about their business. A group of young, fresh faced soldiers wearing oversized hats and long coats march along the pavement. It feels like the 1940s. Walking through Kremlyovskaya Square, one of eight squares in the city, we admire the impressive Sophiysky Cathedral. Stalin lived in Vologda while in exile, and we seek out the apartment where he stayed, which is now a real estate office.

In need of a hot shower and a bed for the night, we go in search of the 17th Century Sretenskaya; a church that has apparently been converted into a hostel for students in the Ministry of Culture's study program. We drive along a bumpy unpaved track that runs parallel with the river. The building looks impressive with its whitewashed walls and grey domes. We make our way over to the entrance. The door creaks open and we step inside.

A tall guy with a neatly trimmed beard, who is wearing a red checked shirt and beige corduroy trousers, steps out of a room at the end of the corridor.

'You are looking for a room?' he asks.

'Yes,' I reply.

'There are two beds free. Please follow me.'

We follow him down the wooden corridor and turn into the first room on the left. We peer around the door into what appears to be the kitchen-cum-dining area. It's a small room with two single beds, one pushed up against the wall and the other positioned under the window.

Si frowns. 'Is this the room?'

'Yes, eu, as you can see it is also the communal kitchen.'

A painfully thin girl with short hair stands hunched over an ancient stove as she waits for the kettle to boil, and a scruffy guy sits at a small table in the middle of the room and tucks into a plate of what can only be described as yellow vomit.

'Please, come inside,' the French guy smiles.

We walk around the table and are invited to sit down. The room is dimly lit. I glance over at the light switch and consider turning it on, but decide against it for fear of causing offense. The gaunt girl sits on the edge of the bed beneath the window and begins to merrily pick her toenails.

The French guy grabs a chair and swings it over to us. 'So, where do you come from?' he asks.

'We've driven here from England,' I smile.

'Mon Dieu, you have travelled a great distance. What was your route?'

'Across southern Germany and up through the Czech Republic, Poland and the Baltic States. We stopped in Saint Petersburg last night.'

'Ah, qui, a beautiful city and a beautiful city I know very well. I was there recently and saw an opera at the Mariinsky Theatre. It was incredible. Please, let me introduce myself. My name is Jon-Pierre and these are my friends, Barbara and Carlos, from the Russian studies program.'

The girl smiles vacantly, while the guy eating the vomit simply nods his head.

'I study in Paris and I was born in the Loire Valley. Have you heard of it?'

'Yes, the Troglodyte caves are fantastic,' Si replies.

Jon-Pierre strokes his facial hair. 'Eu, qui, but of course. So, what brings you to Vologda?'

'We're driving to Vladivostok in our Ford Sierra,' I reply.

Jon-Pierre looks confused. 'I am sorry, I do not understand. Why would you drive to Vladivostok?'

'For the adventure,' Si grins.

'I do not think you can do this. You know, Siberia is very big. It is only possible by train.'

'I read in a British newspaper that Vladimir Putin is building a new highway. It's not due for completion for at least seven years, but we thought we'd check it out and see how far we can get.'

Jon-Pierre glances over at Carlos. 'You know about this new road?'

Carlos pauses from eating and shrugs his shoulders.

'I think you are mistaken.'

'It's true,' I nod. 'It's going to be called the Amur highway. When it's completed it will link the Far East with Europe by road for the first time.'

Jon-Pierre looks doubtful. 'I think you have unrealistic dreams. There are wild bears in the Siberian taiga and many bandits. You must have the correct skills to survive in this terrain.'

'Hey, we're not completely incompetent. We're quite knowledge about wilderness survival.'

Si turns to me. 'Are we?'

I lean forward. 'Survival is the art of staying alive. Think of survival skills as a pyramid, built on the foundation of the will to survive.'

Jon-Pierre raises his eyebrows and appears to take interest.

'The next layer of the pyramid is knowledge. It breeds confidence and dispels fears. The third layer is training, mastering skills and maintaining them. To cap the pyramid, add your kit. Combine the instinct for survival with knowledge, training and kit and you will be ready for anything.'

Silence cries out around the room. Even Carlos stops eating his vomit and peers over. Jon-Pierre clears his throat and straightens his posture.

Si laughs. 'Where did you learn that?'

'From John Wiseman.'

'Who is this wise man?' Jon-Pierre asks.

'John wrote the SAS Survival Guide. He was a solider in the British Special Forces for twenty-six years. His balls are made of steel.'

'Heavy,' Si enthusiastically nods.

Jon-Pierre takes a sip of coffee. 'I wish you luck. Your bravery will most certainly be rewarded by this adventure, and, eu, your beautiful journey will take you through small Siberian communities locked away in the dark past of the Soviet Empire.'

Disturbed by the clatter of pots, I open my eyes to a room buzzing with activity. It's early morning and Jon-Pierre butters toast by the sink, Barbara sits at the table and picks her toenails, Carlos is hunched over a fresh plate of yellow vomit and some other guy with long greasy hair and glasses, who just looks weird, stares at me from the doorway. It takes me a few seconds to work out what exactly is going on, then, it occurs to me that I'm lying in a bed in the kitchen-cum-dining-room surrounded by a bunch of freaks. It's cold and dark in the room, but I can just about see daylight through the net curtains.

Jon-Pierre doesn't look happy. 'Bonjour Chris, how are you this morning?'

I sit up and lean against the wall, feeling a little

uncomfortable.

'You look hungover,' he smirks, taking a small delicate bite out of a piece of toast.

'We had a few drinks last night at the Vologda Hotel.'

'Yes, my room is next door.'

Ignoring Jon-Pierre, I turn and catch Barbara looking at me strangely. All of a sudden the events of last night come flooding back into my mind. We had drunk way too much at the Vologda Hotel. Si had befriended a group of Russian businessmen at the bar and after challenging them to a game of ten-pin bowling, one of the hotel's many activities, we had become involved in a highly competitive drinking game. We lost pretty severely and, stumbling back to the church dorm in the early hours, we crashed through the main door and proceeded to play 'Guns N' Roses' tunes with the creaky floorboards. I struggle to pull on my jeans inside my sleeping bag. It's all very embarrassing, and I smile as everyone in the room eats their breakfast and watches the circus monkey getting dressed. I eventually manage to get myself looking semi-decent and despite my t-shirt being on the wrong way round and inside out, I stumble across the room and wake Si. We gather all of our belongings together and head for the door. Carlos, Barbara and the weird dude with the long hair and glasses follow us outside. Waving farewell to a party of blank faces, I toot the horn and accelerate down the track.

* * *

Chris sits hunched over the steering wheel as we head south towards Yaroslavl on the M8. Travelling deep into the rural countryside of European Russia, we pass through a chain of picturesque villages. Pretty blue and green

Hansel and Gretel style houses (made from wood rather than gingerbread) line the roadside, with intricately carved shutters around each of the many small windows. Hard-faced women wearing headscarves and floral print dresses carry heavy buckets of grain and water for the livestock. With their thick black stockings and rubber boots, they look like peasant farmers' wives from an age gone by. At this time of day there are very few men around, apart from the occasional old boy staggering along the roadside all hunched over and wearing a suit jacket that certainly pre-dates World War II.

After a few hours on the road we eventually reach the city of Yaroslavl, which sits to the east of the golden ring surrounding Moscow. Crossing a bridge over the Volga River, we see more domed churches and head east towards the industrial city of Ivanovo. Winding down narrow country lanes, we chase an old guy on a rusty moped and find our way back onto a red road. Chris fiddles with the radio and finds a station playing Russian jazz. We lose ourselves in the drive and I begin to feel more relaxed than I have felt since leaving England. Our worries of getting the Sierra into Russia are no longer a concern and with thousands of miles of tarmac ahead of us before we reach the frontier of our journey, there is little left to do except switch off and simply enjoy our existence.

Driving for much of the day, we eventually reach Ivanovo in the early afternoon. Passing a large industrial power plant in the ugly concrete suburbs, I become confused by the lack of road signs directing us through the city. Approaching a busy junction I hesitate for a second, unsure whether to turn left or right. The impatient driver of the car behind blasts his horn, and the commotion draws the attention of a police officer leaning against his police jeep. He immediately signals for us to pull over.

I climb out of the driver's seat and brace myself for some trouble. The police officer swaggers over and barks at me in Russian. I haven't time to scan through the phrasebook, and he gives up waiting for a reply and snatches the documents out of my hand. He begins flicking through my passport and finds the page with my photograph and makes brief eye contact before asking me another question in Russian.

I shrug my shoulders and grin helplessly. 'Nyet Rooskee.'

Shaking his head, he gestures for me to follow him over to his police vehicle. Opening the door to the old jeep, he flips the front seat forward and I climb into the back. He climbs behind the wheel and mutters something to the young cop in the front passenger seat. They both look at me and continue to exchange comments to each other in Russian. While the officer studies the car documents, I take the opportunity to open the phrasebook and turn to the page of useful phrases. He waves my passport in the air and starts shouting at me again. I look at him blankly and he begins to laugh. Removing a wallet from his jacket, he shows me a fifty-ruble note and I assume he wants money. Unprepared to argue, I pull a few crumpled notes out of my pocket and handover two twenties and a ten, which amounts to roughly one pound sterling. This appears to relieve the tension a little. Showing him the phrasebook, I point to the word for "tourist". He laughs again, and the young fresh-faced rookie sitting next to him looks at me with intrigue. The older cop's face is weather-beaten, and from the many deep lines running across his forehead and down his cheeks, it's clear he likes to smoke the occasional cigarette and knock back the odd vodka or two. He grabs the phrasebook out of my hand and points to the word "nationality".

'Oh, uh, English,' I reply.

'Ah, Britaniya,' he laughs, 'how-do-you-do?'

Cracking a smile, I reach over and shake his hand. 'How-do-you-do, too?'

This breaks the ice and we all begin to laugh.

'David Beckham,' the young cop chips in.

'Yes, David Beckham,' I reply.

He ejects a tape from out of the cassette player. 'Rok moozika,' he beams, handing it to me.

This sparks off the other cop, who reaches inside the glove box and fishes out a packet of banana flavoured condoms. He hands them to me and I study the packet with keen interest.

'Boom-boom,' the older officer laughs with wide eyes.

This really amuses them and we all begin to slap our thighs and laugh in unison. I open my wallet and whip out two condoms. Fascinated, they both study the writing on the packet and return grateful smiles. All of a sudden another police vehicle pulls up beside us, and the older cop looks serious for a minute as he talks to his colleague. He starts the engine and moves the jeep closer to the Sierra. Pointing at me and then at our car, he suggests we follow him. I jump out and slip behind the wheel.

'It's okay, they're not the GAI. They want us to follow them. I think they're going to help us get out of the city. They gave me a packet of banana flavoured condoms.'

Chris's eyes light up. 'Excellent.'

Striking the engine, I indicate right at the junction and the cop overtakes and pulls out into the road. He puts on his blue flashing lights and we're given a police escort through the city.

'This is insane,' Chris laughs, buzzing with excitement.

'Hey, they also gave me a Russian rock music tape. Try

and remove that road trip compilation that's stuck in the cassette player.'

Chris forces a pen inside the tape slot, and wiggling it around vigorously he manages to pop it out. Following the cop's lead, I turn left into a small car park next to a rundown café. We pull up next to the police jeep and jump out of the car. The cops walk over to the Sierra and study our vehicle.

'Ford,' the older cop nods, peering through the window.

Grabbing the road trip tape from the dashboard, I hand it to the younger cop. He slots it into the jeep's stereo and turns up the volume. 'Black Velvet' blasts from the speakers and the two cops bop their heads in time with the music. After our little music session, we all step inside the small canteen. Everyone stops talking and looks over at us, but I feel safe in their company. We sit outside on a picnic bench beneath a green tarpaulin roof. The waitress appears with a tray of hot dogs and coffees. I whip out my wallet, but the older cop shakes his head and insists that he pay. Squirting mayonnaise onto our hot dogs, we all look at each other between mouthfuls of food and nod in agreement that it tastes good. Opening up the atlas on the table, Chris shows them our route from England on the map. They're fascinated by our journey, and seem puzzled how we transported the car across the water from England to France. The older cop picks up the phrasebook and studies it for a while before pointing to the word "destination".

'Vladivostok,' Chris replies, sipping his coffee.

They look at each other in amazement.

The older cop points to Vladivostok on the map. 'Da?'

I nod. 'Da.'

They grin at each other and exchange comments. I find

the word for "married" and point to the cops. The young rookie has a baby and the older guy has three daughters.

I look up the word for "brother" and point at Chris.

'Brat?' The young kid frowns.

'Da.'

They both look surprised. I consider telling them we're twins, but decide not to overcomplicate things.

Finishing the coffees we return to our vehicles. The older cop quickly presents us with half a bottle of Russian vodka and his policeman's hat. The younger cop follows suit and removes his police tiepin and clips it to my fleece. Chris digs out a few English coins and a postcard of our hometown. He writes a message on it thanking them for their hospitality. The older cop responds by taking the pen and writing in Russian "from the Ivanovo police department" down the side of the bottle of vodka. Putting on their blue flashing lights, they escort us out of the city and encourage us to fill up an empty bottle from an ancient water pump. Shaking their hands in turn we bid them a final farewell. Buzzing from the experience of drinking coffee and eating hot dogs with two Russian cops, we head off on our journey once more. With fresh legs, we drive south on the Volga Highway (M7) to Vladimir before turning east towards Nizhny Novgorod, Russia's fifth largest city. Located at the confluence of the Oka and the Volga River, we pass through the bustling streets and observe its citizens milling around shops and market stalls. Once known as "Gorky" after the writer Maxim Gorky, Nizhny has for a long time been considered the economic and cultural centre of the vast Volgo-Vyatsky region, and was among several newly founded towns that escaped Mongol devastation.

Finding our way back onto the M7, we continue along the Volga and visit countless villages and tiny rural communities. Grumpy faced women sell apples in multi-coloured plastic buckets at the roadside, and we avoid horse-drawn carts as farmers make the journey home after a long hard day at market. Hurtling into the early evening, the sun begins to break through the clouds and we push deeper into Russia towards the city of Kazan. Caught behind an old red Lada with a mountain of sheep's wool strapped to its roof like an enormous blonde afro-wig, Chris overtakes and we join a convoy of trucks transporting goods east. The sun slowly sinks below the horizon and floods the interior of the car in beautiful golden light. We pull over for the night at a truck stop outside of Kazan and watch Russia fade to black.

Chasing the Trans-Siberian

My sleeping bag is wet on the outside and my breath is clearly visible. I turn on the heater, but quickly flick it off again when I'm blasted in the face by cold air. We're sandwiched between two trucks from Kazakhstan that tower above the Sierra. Si collapses out of the car and boils a pan of water on the gas stove. The truck stop is eerily quiet. With a slight chill in the air, I pull up my collars and glance across the fields through a morning mist.

Keen to get moving while it's still early we embark on a 200-mile journey to Perm, an industrial city slap-bang on the Trans-Siberian Railway line. Cutting across the lush green landscape on the pothole infested E22 highway, I grit my teeth when Si hits one particular deep crater with extreme force. We can see the Ural Mountains on the horizon; a geological boundary between Europe and Asia, which stretch low for 1,250 miles from Kazakhstan to the Arctic Kara Sea in the north. Containing huge quantities of metals and minerals, the Urals have been vital to Russia's economy for almost three hundred years, and were described rather accurately by writer, Colin Thubron as "a faint upheaval of pine-darkened slopes".

We journey into the Volga Region and witness more ancient villages occupied by small one-storey houses that are constructed from timber with corrugated roofs. Russian grandmothers "babushkas" wearing headscarves sell multi-coloured feather dusters to the passing traffic. Crossing the Kama River near the city of Perm, a passenger train hauls its carriages across a beautifully designed Metal Truss Railroad Bridge. It occurs to me it could be the Trans-Siberian closing in on Moscow after its epic 9,300km journey from Vladivostok in the Far East of Siberia. This world famous train line was built across the most challenging territory, and it is considered to be one of the great engineering feats of the 19th Century. Tsar Alexander III gave the project his official sanction in 1886 with the curious words, "It is time, high time!"

Perm, a city founded in 1723, is twinned with Oxford in the United Kingdom. It was a restricted area of Russia during the Soviet years and a 'closed city' until 1989. Barbed wire fences once surrounded the periphery with armed guards and, due to its remote location deep in the Urals, Perm was chosen to be the centre for Soviet tank production. During Stalin's regime, the city had also become the location of one of the many horrendous Gulag forced labour camps in Russia and Siberia. Founded in 1943 the "Perm-36" camp operated for more than 40 years, serving until 1953 as a typical logging camp found throughout the country. After Stalin's death, the camp was converted to a prison for those accused of organising "groundless repressions" under the Stalinist regime, and from 1972 until 1988 it operated as the harshest political camp in the country. There was a special regime facility here (the only one of its kind in the country) that housed political prisoners in twenty-four-hour closed cells.

Becoming lost, we follow a long straight road that runs parallel with a towering brick wall with barbed wire on the top. It appears to be a military base. Two guards clutching large automatic rifles look suspiciously in our direction. Agreeing it's probably wise not to hang around we return swiftly to the main road and make our way towards the city centre. We drive along the wide tree-lined avenues, where 19th Century mansion buildings stand next to ugly concrete tower blocks. Countless little kiosks line the pleasant streets, where Georgians and Armenians sell their original spicy kebabs and shoarmas straight from the barbecue. I see a guy with a dark complexion and thick black stubble selling jewellery. He looks to be of Tatar ethnicity. Trolleybuses zoom around at speed, and we take a stroll around the squares and parks and wander down Lenin Street that is busy with local Perm residents (Permyaks). I take photos of the famous Perm Opera and Ballet House and we devour a dish of Pelmeni dumplings, while enjoying the knowledge that the city was the setting for Boris Pasternak's controversial 1950s epic novel Doctor Zhivago. In the book, Perm was the fictional town of Yuriatin. The novel had been refused publication under the USSR due to its independent minded stance on the October Revolution. Controversially, the US Central Intelligence Agency had intercepted a copy of the manuscript that had been smuggled to Milan and arranged for a Russian-language edition of the manuscript to be published and distributed at the Vatican pavilion at the 1958 Brussels world's fair. Further more, it was claimed by historian Ivan Tolstoi that the CIA had lent a hand to ensure that Doctor Zhivago was submitted to the Nobel Committee in its original language in order for Pasternak to win the Nobel Prize for literature. This, of course, had the desired affect of harming the international credibility of the Soviet Union.

A rusty obelisk with the emblem of the hammer and sickle zips by as we battle through the industrial city. Si flicks on the radio and we listen to some funky Russian music, but our moment of road trip heaven is suddenly cut short when I notice a GAI officer up head waving his black and white baton in the air. I pull over and the machine gun wielding traffic cop flicks through our documents. He peers inside the Sierra and then orders me to get out of the car. After rummaging through our worn out possessions in the trunk he commands me to close it. He then gestures for me to follow him over to a concrete control tower. I glance at his automatic rifle and wonder if it's an AK-47. Leading me up a flight of concrete steps to a small control room, a stocky police officer with a shaved head spins around on his swivel chair. He is wearing military camouflage and is sitting at a desk in front of a row of old fashioned black and white CCTV monitors. He scans through the car documents and studies the business visa in my passport. He asks me a question and I randomly attempt to guess what he's asking.

'Road trip, Vladivostok,' I smile, pointing east and using both of my hands to imitate steering an imaginary car.

The two guys look at each other and laugh. I can feel my face burning bright red with embarrassment. He once again flicks through the pages of my passport and appears impressed by the number of stamps and visas from around the world. With an almost respectful nod, he hands me the documents and says something that sounds soft and pleasant. I quickly shake their hands and sprint back to the car.

We chase the Trans-Siberian railway line towards Yekaterinburg, a city 41km inside Asia. The sun begins to set behind us in the west as we cut across the gently undulating Ural Mountains on the only road going east, the only road to Vladivostok. Tearing open a packet of chocolate biscuits, I'm about to pop one in my mouth when Si points out blue-flashing lights up ahead. I slow right down and it becomes clear it's not a GAI checkpoint this time, but instead a head on collision involving a brown Lada and a white saloon car. The vehicles have been crushed beyond recognition and both window screens have been smashed out. I weave around the sharp debris in the road and two police officers stand beside the body of a bald middle-aged man, who lies outstretched on the tarmac. His face is grey and covered in lacerations. Inside the white saloon, I can see the shape of someone slumped over the steering wheel. Russia has one of the highest road accident rates in the world, with an average of 520 incidents every day with 700 people being injured and 95 killed. 34,000 people died in more than 208,000 road traffic accidents in 2002, that's a massive figure especially when there are only 147 million people living in such a vast country. You only have to see the many crosses at the roadside to understand the magnitude of the problem they have here. So many young people, innocent children and families lost. I feel a little shaken, particularly as this is the first time I have seen a dead body. Only half an hour ago the brown Lada overtook us at great speed. I remember cursing the driver and wondering what's the rush? Now he's dead, lying there motionless - the life removed from his body. Throughout his whole life this man has not known when he will die, he's probably thought about it, we all do, but finally that day has arrived. It's an image I will never forget.

As the light begins to fade we stumble across a roadside café. Inside the small wooden building, a guy with dark skin and jet-black hair is standing behind the counter. We study the menu pinned to the wall and point at a couple of dishes in the hope that it will be something edible. Si points to a fridge and orders a couple of beers. Four men chat loudly on the table behind. The senior member of the group looks unlike anyone I have seen before. His face is long and he has an enormous nose. A thick grey moustache hangs from his top lip and his complexion is also dark. It occurs to me that they could be the Kazakh people living in Russia along the Kazakhstan border. They are of Turkic descent and are closely related to the Kyrgyz and the Karakalpak. The Kazakh are the second largest Muslim group in Central Asia, and developed a distinct ethnic identity in the late 15th and 16th centuries. They were the most influential of the various Central Asian ethnic groups, but the Russian Civil War of the 1920s and 1930s, killed half of the population forcing many to flee to China and Mongolia. Since the collapse of Soviet communism, the Kazak have been searching for their identity. Traditionally, they were nomadic shepherds; however, under Soviet rule, much of their land was seized and used for collective farming. As industry developed, their economy and culture became dependent entirely on the Russians.

By the time we receive our food, which turns out to be a gigantic spicy sausage served with a variety of cold beans and lashings of olive oil, I begin to feel quite drunk. Studying the label on the back of the bottle, I notice the beer we're drinking has an alcohol content of 8%. It helps to block out the awful image of the car accident, so we quickly order two more. Paying for our food, I ask the guy if it's ok to sleep in the car outside his café. He seems to understand my sign language and raises his thumb. We bid him goodnight and retire to the car feeling happy to be alive, but equally plagued by the thought of the dangers that lie ahead.

*\ *\ *

After an uncomfortable night's sleep, we head cautiously over the last of the Ural Mountains towards the city of Yekaterinburg, the birthplace of Boris Yeltsin and a major stop on the Trans-Siberian Railway. Chris seems happy for me to drive, and I wonder if he's still shaken after seeing the car accident yesterday. Approaching the brow of a hill, I grit my teeth at the thought of a truck hurtling towards us on the wrong side of the road. Fortunately, we make it to the outskirts of the city intact, and feel greatly relieved to see signs of civilisation. We pass tall buildings eight stories high, displaying huge posters of fashion models advertising jewellery, perfume and designer sunglasses. You can see the city is booming from the Urals mineral wealth. Yekaterinburg is the capital of Siberia and the fourth largest city in Russia, and it was here where the Bolsheviks executed Tsar Nicholas II and his family in 1918. We pass the newly constructed Church on the Blood, at the supposed site of the execution of Tsar Nicholas II. In the 1990s Yekaterinburg was a hotbed of criminal activity, earning itself a name as The Gangster Capital of Russia. The Uralmash and the Central Group were at war, and the most famous "gangster graves" in Russia are in Yekaterinburg. The city's Uralmash cemetery is the resting-place of many of the mobsters killed in a 90s gun battle between rival gangs for control of strategic resources. Following tramlines and trolleybuses into the city centre with its huge shopping malls, hotels and juice bars, I battle with the nightmare traffic and spot a cash machine.

Chris stays with the car while I jump out and wait patiently behind a smartly dressed couple. As they turn to leave, I point at the cash machine.

'Is it working?' I ask, hoping they will understand what I am saying.

'Yes, you have Visa?' the guy replies in near perfect English.

'No, Cirrus.'

The guy studies the card, and shrugs. 'Hmm, I think this machine will not take Cirrus.'

'Do you know where I can change Euros?'

'It's Sunday, the banks are closed. You could try one of the big hotels.'

'Is there one near here?'

He scratches his stubble and converses with the woman with strawberry blonde hair standing beside him. 'We can take you there if you like. You have car?'

'Yes.'

'Please follow me.'

After a short drive, we turn into the car park of the impressive Atrium Palace Hotel. We follow the guy inside the huge glass building, and make our way over to a woman standing behind the reception desk. He asks her a question, but she replies with a shake of her head.

'The money exchange is closed,' he sighs. 'It re-opens at one o'clock.'

'We don't mind waiting for a couple of hours,' I reply.

'I am sorry I could not do more. It is Sunday.'

'No, really, we're very grateful for all your help.'

'Where are you from?' he asks.

'England.'

'London?'

'Very near.'

'I have been to London two times on business. I work for an oil company here in Yekaterinburg. I like Soho and Camden Market very much. So, you have driven here from England?'

'Yep, all the way,' Chris replies proudly.

'This is amazing. Where do you go now?'

'We're heading for Vladivostok,' I smile.

The guy laughs. 'You drive to Vladivostok? You are comedian, yes?'

I shake my head vehemently. 'No, we really are on our way to Vladivostok. Why doesn't anybody believe us?'

'But there is no road. It is impossible to drive there.'

I frown. 'But I read about the construction of a new road called the Amur highway.'

'This is Russia, my friend, never believe what you read. It takes a long time to get things done here. They have been talking about this project for over thirty-eight years. There is no road. It is all lies. You can put your car on the train.'

'Are you sure about that?'

'Yes, many people put their vehicle on the train.'

'No, I mean about there not being a road.'

The guy looks at us strangely. 'I am sorry to give you bad news. It seems incredible that you travel this far without knowing. Putin once talked about building a road between Chita and Khabarovsk, linking Europe with Asia. His goal was to have it completed in eight years. But it is all dreams. Once again, I am sorry to have ended your plans.'

'It's not your fault,' I smile. 'Thanks for taking the time to help us.'

The guy glances down at his watch. 'I must go now. My girlfriend's mother is cooking lunch.'

'No problem, it was very nice meeting you. Thanks again.'

We shake the guy's hand and watch him march out of the building.

'That's it, then. Our journey is well and truly over.'

I nod. 'Certainly looks that way.'

'Bollocks!' Chris yells.

The girl on reception glances over, so we trudge back to the car.

I slump behind the wheel and release a deep sigh. Flipping open the road atlas I follow the route along the Trans-Siberian Railway line. We're exactly halfway above Kazakhstan. There are still five more time zones to cross before we reach Vladivostok. I continue to trace the route with my finger towards Omsk and Novosibirsk. Travelling above the Altai Mountains the road winds through the never ending forests of Siberia, dips down close to the border with Mongolia, loops around the bottom of the colossal Lake Baikal and comes to a halt at the city of Chita in the Far East.

Leaping out of the car, I show Chris the road atlas. 'Do you know what I think?'

Chris casts me a sideways glance. 'Go on.'

'We should just keep on going! That was always the idea, right? I mean, we didn't even know if the Sierra was going to make it to Estonia, let alone Yekaterinburg. I definitely read on the internet that there is about three hundred and fifty kilometres of highway still under construction. Surely there must be a way through.'

'Maybe you're right. Maybe we should just keep going until we run out of road.'

'Exactly, brother, Vladivostok or bust! We've got absolutely nothing to lose.'

Chris beams with excitement. 'Hey, Si, if we make it to Vladivostok I'm going to buy you a beer.'

'A beer? If we make it to Vladivostok we're going to need a crate.'

Bandits & Butterflies

With rubles bursting out of our pockets, Si confidently drives through the city of Tyumen; a business capital where during World War II Lenin's body was secretly hidden from the invading Germans. Like the Trans-Siberian we head east, and skid onto the P402 to Omsk. It's a long and empty road with wide open grass plains stretching out into the distance. We chase telegraph poles that link arms in a line for hundreds of miles. Occasionally, we catch a glimpse of the Trans-Siberian cutting across the landscape and we feel reassured that if all fails at least we can catch the train. In the middle of nowhere a microlight glides low overhead, and I imagine it's a rich farmer behind the controls or a crazy Dutchman attempting to fly solo around the world.

We park up for the night at a rest stop 50km outside of Omsk. Sitting at a picnic table outside a café, we're greeted by a woman who informs us she is from Tashkent in Uzbekistan. She's tiny and has a dark brown face and oriental features that are framed by a white Muslim headscarf. The woman serves us fried chicken and plain rice, and she makes us laugh when she stamps her feet with frustration at the mosquitoes nipping around her ankles. She explains in near perfect English that she has two children living in Tashkent and has come to Siberia to work for her uncle for six months. Listening to her with great intrigue, I begin to realise how incredibly ignorant we are about the rest of the world and the level of intelligence of people who are far less privileged than ourselves. She tells us about her long journey from Uzbekistan with her nephew across the perilous mountain roads of Kazakhstan; a journey she has made out of necessity, not by choice as we have. She misses her children terribly, but hopes to put them through school with the money she'll earn working here. Her eldest daughter is six years old and she can already speak a few words in English. We chat and drink into the night before stumbling back to the car.

Si takes the wheel and we hit the open road at sunrise. The weather changes from dark and overcast, to beautiful bright sunshine. In the winter the temperature in Siberia can drop to as low as -50°C, but at this time of year, particularly where we are now, it's as hot as Miami. Before long we enter the Khakassia Republic and Novosibirsk, an important industrial and transport centre between the coalfields and the mineral deposits of the Ural Mountains to the west. With a population of over one million people, orange and white high-rise buildings crowd the banks of the Ob River. Cruising through the centre of the city, we pass a huge outdoor market selling car parts. There are literally hundreds of makeshift stalls crammed together side by side selling headlights, car doors, batteries, hubcaps, engines, wheels and car stereos. Si grabs two strong black coffees from a food vender, and we browse the stalls that fill the muddy waste ground. I'm intrigued by the many different faces of the people buying and selling goods. Some people have dark complexions and black hair, others small features and oriental eyes. It feels like we have suddenly been transported to Central Asia and it occurs to me that many of these people may originate or, even still live, in neighbouring Kazakhstan, Uzbekistan and Tajikistan, which used to be part of the USSR. A man with grey hair who is wearing a brown patterned jumper beams a smile and points to a cardboard box full of car headlights. I politely decline and move on to the next stall. A portly chap wearing a t-shirt covered in oil stains sits in a deckchair and reads a newspaper. Car door handles and hub cabs are layed out on a table in front of him. He appears to be too engrossed in news to care about a sale. Despite there being a million things to buy, we head off empty handed with our trainers caked in mud. Leaving the bustling traffic of Novosibirsk on the M53 to Kemerovo, we soon find ourselves on a long empty road. We begin to feel like we're making progress, when Si points out a signpost that reveals we still have a whopping 1,778km to travel before reaching Lake Baikal.

We arrive in Kemerovo around 8 o'clock in the evening. It's a pleasant little town with pavement cafés spaced out either side of the street. Attractive women walk arm-in-arm through the tree-lined avenues, and clean cut guys cruise around the streets in shiny cars. All of a sudden, the engine of the Sierra begins to make a strange vibrating sound. We ignore it at first and turn up the volume on the stereo, but it gradually gets louder and louder until it becomes deafening. The growling tractor noise howls across the town and crowds of people standing outside bars watch in amusement as we roar past. Concerned we may have damaged the engine by putting the wrong grade of fuel in the tank, we pull over by a rundown tyre garage a few miles outside town.

Si finds a length of old hosepipe and feeds one end into the tank.

'Are you sure you know what you're doing?'

He pauses for a second, and looks up at me from behind his long fringe. 'Yes, I have done this before, you know. It doesn't take a genius to syphon petrol out of a car.'

Si takes a deep breath before sealing his mouth around the end of the hose. He sucks vigorously, but turns red and immediately retches before spitting out a mouthful of petrol. I try not to laugh. Clutching his head, he swills his mouth out with water.

'That was disgusting! It's burning the roof of my mouth.' He hands me the hose. 'You try.'

I'm just about to have a go, when I see a shaven-haired guy with a barechest beneath his denim dungarees emerge from the tyre garage. Wearing flip-flops, he casually walks over and peers down at the pipe hanging out of the petrol tank. Si grabs the phrasebook from the car.

'Pamageetee pazhalstra,' the guy mumbles.

I frown. 'What did he say?'

'I don't know,' Si shrugs, flicking through the pages.

The mechanic folds his oily arms and continues to stare down at the pipe. Spinning on his heels he strolls into the garage and returns with a large white plastic container. He places it on the ground and begins sucking on the end of the hose. Within seconds, petrol is gushing out of the pipe and he quickly shoves it into the container. The guy looks up and nods. We both smile, unsure what to say. The plastic container slowly fills with the urine coloured liquid. The last few drops of fuel dribble out of the pipe, and the guy jumps to his feet, wipes his hands on his dungarees and points towards two petrol pumps on the far side of the yard. He walks around the car and studies our registration plate before disappearing back inside the garage.

'Nice guy. He could've charged us for that,' Si grins, screwing on the petrol cap.

'I guess tourists don't pass through these parts all that often. This town isn't a Trans-Siberian stopover.'

Pushing the Sierra over to the petrol pump, we fill up the tank with octane 95. We climb back inside the car and just as we're about to join the road and pick up speed, the tractor noise starts up again. Spinning around, we screech to a halt on the mechanics forecourt. I lift up the hood and peer down at the rusty, oil covered engine. Si reaches inside the car and grabs an ancient copy of a Haynes manual.

'There isn't a section for "strange engine noises",' he sighs, scanning the pages.

I lean through the driver's window and turn the key. The engine jerks into life and begins shaking vigorously from side to side, rattling and ticking and clicking.

'Hey, I think it could be that pipe,' I suggest, pointing at the engine. 'It's disconnected from the main chamber. Hang on, there's a bolt missing!' I smile. 'It was probably shaken loose driving over potholes.'

Si frowns. 'What shall we do?'

'Fix it, I guess.'

'How are we going to do that?'

'We could try bandaging it together with kitchen foil and wire.'

'Are you sure that'll work?'

'Nope.

Pushing the two pieces of pipe together we quickly begin to wrap the foil around the join and, just as I'm about to use some wire to hold it all in place, the mechanic guy from the tyre garage appears behind us. He glances down at our handy work and begins to laugh. He gestures for us to drive the car into his garage workshop. Feeling embarrassed, but happy to accept some assistance from our new friend, we swing the car around and he directs us inside and onto a ramp. After closing the garage doors, the guy points at two wooden stools next to a small table and a stove. We sit down and fight to get comfortable. The mechanic presses a button, and we can hear the sound of hydraulics as the ramp slowly lifts the Sierra a few feet into the air. He jumps down inside the pit and taps the underbelly of the car with a wrench, before peering over the side of the pit and raising his thumb in the air. We both smile and nod reassuringly. Ten minutes later, he climbs out of the pit with oil on his face and indicates to us that the job is complete. We wait patiently for the guy to present us with an enormous bill, but instead he begins to boil the kettle. Picking up a tin of coffee off the floor, he shovels a couple of teaspoons into three stained mugs. He laughs and says something in Russian, but we haven't got a clue what he's talking about, so we just laugh back. We sit in silence for a while, and then he whips his wallet out of his pocket. He flips it open and pulls out a photograph of a pretty young woman holding a baby in her arms. We study the picture with interest. Taking a sip of coffee, I attempt to try out some Russian words from the phrasebook. He laughs and sparks up a cigarette. Heating up a pan of borshch on his small cooking stove, he pours some into two bowls and, for some unknown reason, apart from maybe to break the ice I show him a particularly nasty graze on my left elbow. Si quickly joins in and rolls up his jeans to display a small scar on his knee, but the guy doesn't seem impressed at all and just looks at us strangely. All of a sudden, he stands up and pulls down his dungarees to reveal a massive deep scar on the back of his thigh. We both look at it and gasp. He then mimes firing a machinegun and uses his hands to imitate an explosion.

'Chechnya,' he nods, pointing to his leg.

He grabs a pen and a piece of paper and scribbles down the date 1994. This guy can't be much older than twenty-six, which means he would have only been about seventeen when he went to war in Chechnya. He tries to act out what happened, and it looks like a piece of shrapnel had embedded itself in his leg when a landmine exploded. Many people were killed. He crosses his chest. I feel like an idiot for showing him my graze, and I suddenly realise that it doesn't matter how far we drive across Siberia, very little can measure up to the harsh realities of war. Shaking his head, he quickly lights another cigarette and grabs his diary. Punching a number into his mobile phone, he stands up and shows us a worn out single mattress behind a flimsy divider.

'Dyevachka,' he nods with a smile.

'Dyevachka?'

Si already has his face in the phrasebook. 'Ah, dyevachka means girl.'

'Girl?' I repeat.

'Dyevachka,' the guy winks. He dials another number and points at us and then at the bed.

'He must mean a prostitute,' Si frowns, knocking back his coffee. 'He's dialling a hooker.'

'Are you sure?'

'Well, he's not ordering a pizza, is he?'

I laugh, still trying to comprehend what the hell is going on. 'Wait a minute, let me get this right. Our mechanic buddy is getting a prostitute to come here to the garage?'

'Yes.'

'He can't have sex with a prostitute while we're here. That's just wrong.'

'That seems to be his plan. He probably wants us to pay for it. That's our payment for him helping us out kind of thing. He probably wants us to join in!'

Si quickly turns to the guy and shakes his head. 'Nyet, spaceeba, nyet dyevachka.'

The mechanic's face drops. 'Nyet dyevachka?'

'Da, nyet dyevachka.'

'Nyet dyevachka?'

'Nyet.'

He puts his mobile phone on the table. We sit in silence for a few minutes. Si tries to liven up the mood by asking him more questions from the phrasebook, but he doesn't seem interested. The guy lights another cigarette and stares down at his phone. More silence. We eventually make our excuses and crash out in the car.

* * *

I'm woken by the whirring sound of a machine. I peer out of the window and watch the mechanic skilfully remove a tyre from its rim. Chris is already up and is sitting at the small table sipping coffee from a mug. Climbing out of the car I throw the mechanic a friendly wave. He ignores me and carries on with his job at hand. I assume he is still upset about last night. Feeling as though we have outstayed our welcome we offer him some money for fixing the car, but he declines. We gather together our belongings and say our goodbyes.

It's a beautiful drive to Krasnoyarsk along the potholed M53. The Siberian summer meadows are in full bloom and horses with foals graze peacefully in the lush green fields. Driving a remote stretch of road through the never-ending coniferous forest, we weave around cracks in the tarmac and are reminded of this regions harsh winter temperatures. Accounting for one-fifth of the world's total forested land, the taiga forests are home to pine, spruce and larche and stretch across the high northern latitudes; from here in Russia to Mongolia, Japan, the United States, Canada and Scandinavia. Nowhere else in the world is there such a large population of furry mammals, including bears, weasels, wolves, lynxes, rabbits and squirrels.

After a couple of hours we pass through the town of Mariinsk, a stop on the Trans-Siberian Railway. We pause at the roadside and buy waffles bursting with cream from a friendly babushka. With swollen stomachs we enter the Krasnoyarsk region, which is an astonishing 3,745km from Moscow. Crossing the Chulym River we drop by the old Cossack town of Achinsk, 184km west of Krasnoyarsk. It's yet another stop on the Trans-Siberian Railway line and is one of the oldest known inhabited places in the area. Paleontological study has shown that people lived here as early as 28,000–20,000 BC. The local economy today is based on heavy industry. It has an oil refinery and also produces construction materials, including wood, asphalt and cement. We visit the "Mourning Mother" monument, which was erected fairly recently in honour of the local people who died in the Great Patriotic War from 1941-1945; a war that can only be described as the most ferocious battle in the history of humanity. The Nazi invasion of the USSR in June 1941 ended in complete defeat for Nazi Germany less than four years later with the fall of Berlin on the 9th of May 1945.

We begin to see forested mountains of Siberian pine and birch as we approach the city of Krasnoyarsk. Founded by the Cossacks in 1628, Krasnoyarsk has grown into an industrial centre and is now the largest producer of aluminium in Russia. After the Russian Revolution of 1917, during the periods of centralized planning, numerous large plants and factories were constructed in Krasnoyarsk, including the hydroelectric power station (now the fifth largest in the world and the second biggest in Russia). Krasnoyarsk is also a popular place with painters and people who like to go rafting and climbing. Also, nearby Tuva is one of the few regions in Russia that has retained its ethnical spirit, and is the cultural centre of Shamanism and the "motherland" of throat singing. Wandering around the friendly streets of this exceptionally flat city, where century old mansion buildings stand alongside grey concrete tower blocks, we mooch around the main square and check out the newly constructed "Historical Gates" monument. Author Anton Chekhov described Krasnoyarsk as the most beautiful city in Siberia. He wasn't wrong, especially with the Stolby National Park only a stone's throw away. In 1890, to the amazement of his friends and colleagues, Chekhov made an extraordinary three-month journey across Siberia to the island of Sakhalin off the Pacific Coast to undertake a survey of 10,000 prisoners on the penal colony. It was unlike anything he had done before, and as a long term sufferer of Tuberculosis it called for physical stamina. Chekhov wrote many letters on his Siberia journey.

To His Sister. KRASNOYARSK, May 28, 1890.

"The last three stations have been splendid; as one comes down to Krasnoyarsk one seems to be getting into a different world. You come out of the forest into a plain which is like our Donets steppe, but here the mountain ridges are grander. The sun shines its very best and the birch-trees are out, though three stations back the buds were not even bursting. Thank God, I have at last reached a summer in which there is neither rain nor a cold wind. Krasnoyarsk is a picturesque, cultured town; compared with it, Tomsk is "a pig in a skull-cap and the acme of mauvais ton." The streets are clean and paved, the houses are of stone and large, the churches are elegant.

I am alive and perfectly well. My money is all right, and so are my things; I lost my woollen stockings but soon found them again.

Apart from my trap, everything so far has been satisfactory and I have nothing to complain of. Only I am spending an awful lot of money. Incompetence in the practical affairs of life is never felt so much as on a journey. I pay more than I need to, I do the wrong thing, and I say the wrong thing, and I am always expecting what does not happen.

. . . I shall be in Irkutsk in five or six days, shall spend as many days there, then drive on to Sryetensk - and that will be the end of my journey on land. For more than a fortnight I have been driving without a break, I think about nothing else, I live for nothing else; every morning I see the sunrise from beginning to end. I've grown so used to it that it seems as though all my life I had been driving and struggling with the muddy roads. When it does not rain, and there are no pits of mud on the road, one feels queer and even a little bored. And how filthy I am, what a rapscallion I look! What a state my luckless clothes are in!"

With a backdrop of jagged mountains, we cross the Yenisei River, which starts in Mongolia in the south and flows 3,487km north to the Arctic Kara Sea. Chris scans the horizon for the Anton Chekhov riverboat that supposedly travels up to Dudinka. Ancient nomadic tribes such as the Oghuz tribes and Ket people and the Yugh people lived along the banks of the Yenisei River. The Ket, numbering about 1,000, are the only survivors today of those who originally lived throughout central southern Siberia near the river banks. Their extinct relatives included the Kotts, Assans, Arins, Baikots, and Pumpokols, who lived further upriver to the south. The modern Ket lived in the eastern middle areas of the river before being assimilated politically into Russia during the 17th and 19th centuries. Russians first reached the upper Yenisei in 1605, travelling from the Ob River. During World War II, Nazi Germany and the Japanese Empire agreed to divide Asia along a line that followed the Yenisei River to the border of China, and then along the border of China and the Soviet Union.

We journey deeper into eastern Siberia, and join a convoy of trucks carrying containers with Japanese writing down the side. Up ahead we see a sign for a small truck stop and pay a couple of rubles to use the shower facilities. Feeling fresh, we dump our soiled clothes in the trunk and step inside the café. Claiming a table, we devour a delicious ukha fish soup full to the brim with root vegetables, parsley, leek, potato, bay leaf, dill, tarragon, and spiced with black pepper, saffron, nutmeg and fennel seed. Chris whips out the road atlas and we discuss the route ahead. We're directly above Mongolia now, 483km north of the Altai Mountains and not a huge distance from the Chinese border. This fascinating World Heritage region is steeped in history and legend. In Turkic and Mongolic languages, the name, Altai, means the "Golden Mountain" and this complex mountain system in Central Asia extends 1,200 miles (2,000km) from the Gobi Desert to the West Siberian Plain. Bridging the borders of China, Mongolia, Russia, and Kazakhstan, it is a mosaic of mountains, taiga coniferous forests, steppe and alpine meadows. The Altai-Sayan eco-region is one of the last remaining untouched areas of the world, with snow leopards, wolves, lynx and brown bears roaming the northern parts. The Altai Mountains were once home to the Oghuz "tribe" Turks, who over many centuries migrated west across Central Asia to the Caspian Sea, the Caucasus and Turkey (where they eventually founded the Ottoman Empire). The Altai Mountains have been identified as being the point of origin of a cultural enigma termed the Seima-Turbino Phenomenon, which arose during the Bronze Age around the start of the 2nd millennium BC. It led to a rapid and massive migration from the region into distant parts of Europe and Asia.

Wiping our plates clean, Chris drives towards Irkutsk along the M53 highway that's a cloud of white butterflies. They flutter in their thousands towards the window screen. Some get sucked inside the engine and splat on the front grill, while others fly through the windows and dance around our heads. We pull over and look in awe at these white winged creatures, as they gather on the warm tarmac in monstrous heaps like confetti. Scooping up a pile in my hands, they tickle my face and get caught in my hair. Thundering through the white blizzard of insects for hundreds of miles, we pass through tiny villages similar to the ones we had seen in European Russia with small wooden houses with beautifully carved shutters; some blue, some green. Women wearing brightly coloured headscarves draw water from ancient wells while goats chew on wild flowers. We wait at a rail crossing and wave at a young kid, who zips by in the open carriage of a freight train. The wind blows freely in his hair and he returns our wave as he disappears on his adventure across the top of Asia. We pass through the small town of Kansk in Krasnoyarsk Krai on the Trans-Siberian Railway line, which was founded in 1628 as a Russian fort. The town is a centre of the Kansk-Achinsk lignite basin, which in the early 1980s was developed into one of the largest coal areas of the Soviet Union. After the small villages of Nizhniy Ingash and Tayshet we head deeper and deeper into the wilderness, with 85km until the next village of Nizhneudinsk. Failing to pass a single car on the highway, I look in surprise at a man standing in the middle of the road. He waves his arms urgently above his head and indicates for us to pull over. Chris dabs the brakes and slows down as we approach him. The guy runs over and talks urgently in Russian. He's slightly unshaven, but is smartly dressed in a lime green silky shirt and cream trousers.

'Nyet Rooskee. We don't speak Russian,' I smile, turning off the engine.

'You speak English?'

'Yes, we're from England,' I sing, intrigued to meet a fellow English speaker all the way out here in the middle of Siberia.

'You have petrol?' he asks. 'We no petrol. Breakdown.'

'Of course,' I cheerily reply, happy to assist a fellow traveller in need.

I jump out and meet the guy at the back of the Sierra. As I open the trunk, I notice a kid leaning against a navy blue car on the opposite side of the road.

'I am from Slovenia,' the guy beams, shaking my hand. 'You know my country?'

'It's near Croatia, isn't it?' I reply handing him the petrol can.

He nods. 'You know the world very much.'

The guy's mood quickly changes and he begins to look shifty. He can't quite seem to keep still and glances suspiciously up and down the long empty road, almost checking to see if the coast is clear. I sense something is not quite right. The guy begins to talk urgently at me. He explains how they have run out of petrol and cannot afford to buy more. He's a powerful guy with the most unusual emerald green eyes, and for a second I find myself listening to his sob story. My mind races and I realise where the conversation is heading. I stop him in mid-sentence and tell him we don't have any money. He pulls a gold ring out of his pocket that is mounted with a large red rock. He tells me it's a ruby.

'Please, maybe you buy ring, very cheap, very beautiful.'

He thrusts the ring close to my face and glances up and down the road. He reaches around to his back pocket.

'You buy ring!' the guy cries.

My survival instincts kick in and I slam the trunk shut and sprint around to the driver's door. Leaping inside, I strike the engine and the guy runs around to the passenger window.

'You buy ring!' he shouts, his face red with anger.

I rev the engine and accelerate away at speed.

'What about our petrol can?' Chris yells, looking back at the guy standing in the road.

'Fuck the petrol can. Are they following us?' I cry, checking the rear view mirror. 'He was going to rob me. That guy was actually going to rob me. He started trying to sell me this ring, but I could see in his eyes that he was about to do something.'

'I can't believe you actually got out of the car, it's the first fucking rule. That's why people travel in convoy around here.'

We both eventually calm down and concentrate on making some distance. Chris takes over the driving, and we agree to continue on until it gets dark. The never ending forests and the beautiful meadows of the Siberian countryside begin to disappear. Grey smog hangs heavily in the air, blocking out the sun. We pass through a small industrial town that consists of little more than a grotty housing estate and a rundown processing plant. Rusty pipes loop above the road and kids with grubby faces peer at us as we pass by. On the edge of town, we spy a café with a few trucks parked up outside. It's the first place we have seen in hours, and feeling tired and hungry we decide to check it out. I notice two men and a woman loitering outside the gateway to another enormous factory. Entering the canteen, I'm immediately struck by how thick the steel bars are that stand between ourselves and the woman slouched behind the counter. They look like they belong to an 18th Century jail cell. I hold up the handwritten menu to the bars and point at a couple of different options. Having learnt a few words, I also ask for borshch (beetroot soup with vegetables and meat), khlyeba (bread) and kartofel (potatoes). The gaunt woman, with a starched white cloth tied around her head and bright red lipstick, scowls at us. We walk across the dimly lit room and sit at a large metal table in the corner. The hard-faced male clientele sit hunched over steaming plates of food. I go in search of the bathroom and poke my head inside one of the cubicles. Fishing tissue paper out of my pocket, I lift up the lid and look in surprise when I see a hypodermic needle lying on top of a pile of black shit. I race out of the cubicle and within seconds I'm sitting back at the table.

'There's a used needle in the toilet,' I whisper, stealing glances around the café.

Chris frowns. 'What kind of needle?'

'Someone around here is jacking up. It must be heroin.'

'I didn't know they used that stuff out here?'

'It's probably making its way from Afghanistan.'

The woman behind the counter slides a steel metal tray beneath the bars. The food looks disgusting and we half-heartedly push the inedible mush around our plates for a while. We decide to leave and head back to the car. Locking ourselves inside the safety of the Sierra, we watch the truckers leave the café one by one until the car park is completely empty. After a while the lights inside the café go out. Feeling incredibly vulnerable, we try to block out our surroundings by getting some shut eye, which is impossible as I've got images of the Slovenian guy still haunting my mind. A black shape moves behind the Sierra. I nudge Chris awake and peer out into the darkness.

'What is it?' he grumbles, poking his head out of his sleeping bag.

'I just saw something moving outside,' I whisper.

'You're imagining it.'

'I'm not. Someone's out there.'

'It's probably the Grim Reaper coming to get you,' Chris laughs.

'Those highway robbers could've followed us here.'

'Go to sleep.'

I check all of the doors are locked before pulling my sleeping bag tightly around my neck. My heart pounds inside my chest, and just as I'm about to close my eyes I see the black shape flash by my window.

'Right, sod this!' I cry, springing up in my seat. 'There's definitely someone out there!'

Chris unzips his sleeping bag and looks around with wide eyes. 'I can't see anything,' he sighs.

Shadows from the trees blowing in the wind dance across the gravel car park. Suddenly, a hand slaps against my window. We both scream in fear. The drawn and twisted face of a woman with long greasy hair stares at us like a vampire. She has glazed and bloodshot eyes. She quickly disappears.

'What the hell. Start the car!' Chris yells.

I rip open my sleeping bag and fumble in my pocket for the car keys. The woman lunges from out of the darkness and reappears at Chris's window. She tries frantically to open the door.

'Drive,' Chris whispers.

I pull the keys out of my pocket, but they drop down into the footwell. I search desperately for them around the pedals. My dancing fingers finally seize hold of them and I fumble to put the key into the ignition.

Chris leans over and screams in my face. 'Fucking drive!'

Striking the engine the Sierra roars with anger. Flicking on the headlights, the woman runs at the car and begins to hit the window screen repeatedly with her hand. Reversing at speed, I skid out onto the main road and slamming the Sierra into first gear we wheel spin into the night.

Pearl of Siberia

I look in surprise at a large grey Ural owl perched in a tree no more than ten metres away from the car. It watches me curiously, and I wonder if it has been guarding over us during the night. The powerful bird opens its wings and swoops low overhead, before disappearing into the forest like a creature from a mystical fairytale. Si sleeps soundly, his head buried deep inside his sleeping bag. Trying not to disturb him, I drive for 50km before pulling over by an old disused railway carriage that has been converted into a café. We board the train and I smile at the fancy wallpaper and frilly tablecloths. We're the only customers at this early hour, so we choose a table and absorb our wonderful surroundings. A friendly woman wearing a green floral print apron serves us traditional Siberian pirogí, dumplings of unleavened dough folded in half moon shaped parcels. Stuffed with meat, potatoes, cheese, cabbage and small sweet berries, the delicious tasting food is topped with fried onion and served with sour cream. Looking out of the window of the train carriage, I try to imagine the many thousands of kilometres it has no doubt clocked up during its lifetime, and the many people it has transported through wind, rain and snow. Si thanks the woman for such a fine feast. She blushes and her rosy cheeks glow with shyness and pride. No questions asked. There's no need to know who we are, we are just two weary travellers stopping off for a bite to eat.

We journey once more through the remote eastern Siberian villages locked away from the outside world. Old women pump water from ancient wells outside wooden houses that have smoking chimneys. A group of children play with a rusty metal hoop, and a girl wearing a pink party frock with ribbons in her hair rocks gently backwards and forwards on a makeshift swing. It must be unimaginably tough living out here during the cold winter months, but as Anton Chekhov observed during his time here, "better to live in Siberia and feel oneself a man of moral worth, than to live in Petersburg with the reputation of a drunkard and a scoundrel." Spotting a GAI checkpoint up ahead we're immediately flagged over. Si hands the officer our passports and shows him Lake Baikal on the map. As I'm driving, he points me in the direction of a small brick building. I head cautiously towards a policeman with a machinegun standing outside the door. It's dark inside the brick building, and I'm instructed to join four other men lined up against the concrete wall. A policeman wearing a dark green uniform sitting behind a wooden desk waves me over. He shoves a paper funnel up to my mouth. He shouts something at me. I obviously don't understand, so I guess and breathe into it. The policeman whips it away from my face and sniffs hard inside the funnel, which personally I can't help thinking is a really bad idea, particularly as I haven't brushed my teeth for a least 24 hours. He screws up his face and sends me away. I'm about to climb behind the wheel when the GAI officer who pulled us over approaches our vehicle. He mumbles something and points up the highway.

Si pokes his head out of the window. 'What's going on?'

'No idea.'

A cop car pulls up in front of us.

Si frowns. 'What have you done now?'

'I haven't done anything. I just breathed into a paper funnel. Surely you can't be arrested for having bad breath.'

The young cop indicates for us to follow him. Fearing the worst, I strike the engine and pull out onto the highway. We continue to follow the police car for about five miles and arrive at a small concrete town that's not even on the map. We pull up outside a tatty police station and reluctantly make our way inside, but instead of being arrested and thrown in jail we're welcomed with open arms by six policemen. The top dog sergeant, who looks like he could kill a lion with his nose hair, walks over and shakes our hands. It's like putting your hand in a vice, but we both do well to fight back the tears. Even the guy locked up in the cell to my right looks through the bars and smiles. I glance around the station and study the main control desk, which looks like it dates back to the 1960s, with big cheesy dials and switches. A big red telephone begins to ring, and an officer picks up the bone shaped receiver and places it to his ear. He looks hilarious, and I try to hide my amusement. The sergeant slides a registration book in front of us and hands me a pen. We write down our names, address and our country of origin while our passports get passed around the room. It seems pretty clear they have never met anyone from England before, so we try to behave as good ambassadors for our country and smile and thank them in Russian at every opportunity. Escorting us out of the station, all of the policemen crowd around the Sierra. Si speedily grabs the atlas and we show them our route on the map. They smile and chatter excitedly. One of them points at the English Channel, and I explain to them that we put the car on a ferry from England to France. They all seem genuinely surprised that it's possible to drive from England to the Far East by road, and shaking our hands we feel like pioneers breaking down boundaries and uniting the world. The sergeant gestures for me to lift the hood and they all check out the engine and nod their heads. It occurs to me that we haven't seen a Ford on the road since St Petersburg, and I get the distinct impression this is the first one these guys have seen. The excitement of seeing the modern world on their doorstep (even though the Sierra is 16 years old) appears to be a positive sign to them of the future. We're led back out of town by the same police car. At one point they put on their blue flashing lights and we jump a long queue of traffic. Putting us back on the main road to Irkutsk, we wave out of the window and sound our horn as we tear back onto the road.

* * *

Passing dozens of old gingerbread style log houses, Chris directs me through the bustling streets of Irkutsk. A mere 70km from Lake Baikal, this historic city is a major stop off on the Trans-Siberian Railway. It was a bustling trading post in the 1700s due to the construction of the Siberian Road, which connected this remote settlement to Moscow. Fur, diamonds and ivory were sent to Irkutsk from all over Eastern Siberia and carried to Mongolia, Tibet and China to trade for tea and silk. Around that time it was a starting point for many great expeditions to the far north and east. The famous trader, Grigory Shelekhov, led one expedition across the Bering Strait into Alaska and down to California, which was referred to locally at that time as the American district of Irkutsk. Taking a celebratory stroll around the main square, we see a western tourist peering up at a statue of Lenin. Chris snaps a photograph of an enormous red communist star and a hammer and sickle rusting away in the centre of a traffic island - an emblem signifying the alliance of workers and peasants. Communism had come and gone, leaving these final reminders behind. Seeing these symbols deteriorating at the roadside, I can only assume they haven't removed them out of nostalgia for those days. I guess it takes time for people to let go of an ideology that dominated their lives for so long, but eventually they too will disappear along with all of their fears of change and worries about the future. The world will move on.

A short drive outside Irkutsk, we're brought to a sudden halt while workmen direct oncoming traffic around a mechanical digger. A police cop approaches a burgundy saloon at the front of the queue. He grabs what appears to be a bottle of beer out of the driver's hand, and we watch in utter bemusement when he takes a swig before handing it back. He playfully pats the driver on the shoulder before waving him on. Driving into thick smog, we travel alongside the Eastern Sayan Mountains towards the legendary Lake Baikal, the "Pearl of Siberia". Chris reads from the guidebook and reveals bears are known to inhabit the forests in this region of Russia. Visibility worsens with every mile and we're unable to see more than seven or eight metres in front of us. Chris points out how ridiculous it seems that this immense body of water, roughly the size of Belgium, is completely hidden from view. Containing twenty percent of the world's total unfrozen freshwater reserves, Baikal has a volume greater than North America's five Great Lakes combined. Forming in a rift valley an astonishing twenty-five million years ago, it is one of the oldest lakes on the planet, with almost all other lakes on earth (including Loch Ness in Scotland) having only been in existence for approximately twenty-five thousand years. Fascinatingly, as a result of its ancient origins the ecology of Baikal is similar to the Galapagos Islands, where animal and plant life have evolved in complete isolation. Of over two thousand recorded plant and animal species found at Baikal over seventy two percent are found nowhere else on earth, and include the Baikal seal and over 60 native species of fish. During the winter months ice on the lake freezes up to a metre thick, so it's used as a temporary road between the remote settlements in the north and the south; a risky short cut when you consider the lake bed is known for being a graveyard of cars and trucks.

We reach the bottom of the mountain and glide alongside a low stone wall.

Chris springs up out of his seat. 'Stop the car! I think I can see water.'

I bring the Sierra to an abrupt halt and we both leap out and race over to the wall. Squinting, I'm unable to see anything.

Chris points into the thick smog. 'Can you see it?'

I catch a glimpse of three ripples no more than ten metres away.

'Is that it?' I sigh, launching a stone into the water. 'We drive thousands of miles across harsh terrain and all we can see are three stupid little ripples.'

Chris nods. 'I'm afraid so. This whole area in front of us must be Lake Baikal.'

'But that's ridiculous. How can you hide a lake the size of Belgium?'

I glance down at the map and see that the M55 hugs

the south eastern shore of the lake for about 320km. We're bound to see an area clear of smoke somewhere along the way. Reaching the small town of Slyudyanka, we pass a group of local fisherman heading for the train station. They mainly catch omul in Baikal, which is a salmon like species of fish. We continue to drive into the fading light without seeing a single ripple. Once past the town of Selenginsk, we stumble across a trucker's café at the top of a steep climb. Smoke continues to fill the air and I observe a family of local Buryats cooking up food at the roadside. The young couple and their son have striking faces with pink rosy cheeks and narrow eyes. The Buryats are an indigenous group of Mongol people who live in the Baikal region. Many of the 500,000 indigenous people here practise Buddhism, which has existed in the East of Russia for centuries. Though Buddhism was officially recognized in Russia by the Empress 'Ekaterina II' in 1741, Buddhists were Christianized by force in the region of Ulan Ude and some Buryats still live completely nomadic lives; living in gers (a portable dwelling) and herding cattle with the changing seasons.

As night falls the temperature plummets. We step inside a wooden café and are welcomed by warmth and delightful aromas. Steam bellows from the busy kitchen, and we sit at a table next to a huge Mongolian truck driver who slurps soup from a bowl. The man has a wispy goatee beard and his straight jet-black hair is tied back in a ponytail. A leather waistcoat stretches tightly over his muscular shoulders. He is the first Mongolian person I have seen and I realise now how Genghis Khan, the legendary warlord who came from this territory, managed to create history's largest land empire in the 13th Century. Ordering food from a friendly woman working in the kitchen, I return to the table with two bowls of steaming dumpling soup and a couple of square slices of pizza.

Chris pops a dumpling into his mouth, and sighs.

'Don't you like it?'

'No, it's delicious. I was just thinking how incredible it is that we haven't seen Lake Baikal. These fires must be absolutely enormous. I was really looking forward to seeing the damn thing.'

'At the end of the day, Chris, it's just a lake.'

'Lake Baikal is more than "just a lake"! It's the Pearl of Siberia. The waters are crystal clear. In places it's possible to see down more than forty metres.'

'You'll have to come back some other time.'

'Good idea, I'll jump in the car one lazy Sunday afternoon and drive the seven thousand miles back here, shall I?'

'Get the train.'

Chris thinks about this for a second. 'That's actually not a bad idea. Maybe I could do it in the winter.'

Over Chris's shoulder, I see a guy enter the café wearing a bright yellow ski jacket. He is in his late fifties and has a mane of silky grey hair hanging down to his shoulders. He looks over at our table and smiles, almost as if he's seen old friends. He grabs a pizza slice from the counter and joins our table.

'Dobry vyechyeer,' he smiles.

'Hello, I mean, dobry,' I reply.

'Where you from?' the guy asks.

'England,' Chris sings, with a little too much enthusiasm.

His eyes light up. 'Ah, The Rolling Stones. I musician, you play guitar?'

'A little,' I smile.

'I play all Russia, Moscow, St Petersburg and one time in Warsaw.'

'Are you still in a band now?' I ask.

'Da,' he nods, sitting down at the table. 'I similar to Keith Richards, I play until dead.'

'Nice one.'

'You in band?' he asks.

I shake my head. 'Not anymore.'

'Why?'

'I don't know. The band fell apart and I never did it again.'

'If in your blood, you must play.'

Chris finishes his last mouthful of soup. 'Is there always smoke here?' he asks.

'Yes, in summer heat big problem, my friend, big fires, many more days.'

Buying the guy a beer, we continue to talk about music and the world. He turns out to be one wise guy, and I'm sure in a past life he would have been a naive Indian chief or a spiritual shaman. Completely in-tune with himself this is a man who refuses to grow old in his mind. I ask him about the road ahead, but he just shrugs and tells us to enjoy the unknown. He reaches across the table and tucks something into my jacket pocket.

'Remember the summer of sixty-nine,' he smiles, and flicking his silver locks over his shoulders he exits the cafe.

We return to the car with a couple more beers. I reach inside my pocket and find a perfectly rolled joint. It's a wonderful sight to see and sparking up the cone before bedtime, we get stoned high above Lake Baikal.

PART 3

Burn Baby Burn

With swollen pasta shell eyes, Si traverses the Selenga River for 480km. We reach the city of Ulan-Ude, which chokes on the same smoke from the forest fires we had encountered soon after leaving Irkutsk. Ulan-Ude is the starting point of the Trans-Mongolian Railway, which embarks on its epic journey through Mongolia to China and the capital city of Beijing. It was founded by the Russians in 1775, and the city's name was later changed to Ulan Uda meaning "Red Gate" in Buryat. The settlement prospered as a major stop on the tea-caravan route from China via Troitskosavsk, and later became a "closed city" during the Soviet years until 1991. Scanning the inevitable concrete suburban sprawl, I grin into the eerie smog and observe a smart local Buryat gentleman wearing a navy blue suit. Kept on our toes by the small Chinese or Korean minibuses that speed through the historic centre, Si points out a row of merchant houses decorated with carved wood and stone. We take a little stroll to the central square and we're absolutely amazed when we stumble across the largest bronze head in the world 'Lenin's Head'. Built in 1970 for the centennial of Lenin's birth, it towers over the main plaza at 7.7 meters (25 ft) and weighs 42 tons. I try to imagine what my head would look like in its place, and quickly erase this frightening image from my mind. Buying some spicy food from a local Buryat woman with a sweet smile, it occurs to me how friendly she is in comparison to the people we had met in European Russia. The Buryat's are predominantly Buddhist, and located a few kilometres outside the city is the largest Buddhist monastery in Russia. The first known occupants of this region were the Evenks, an indigenous people of the Russian North. Traditionally, they were a mixture of pastoralists and hunter-gatherers, who relied on their domesticated reindeer for milk and transport. In the 17th Century, the Russian Empire began to expand and came into close contact with these remote Evenkis, and in 1666 the Russian Cossacks soon dominated the region and settled in Ulan-Ude. Later the Buryat Mongols, a much larger group, numbering today around 500,000 people, migrated to the area from the Lake Baikal Region.

Leaving civilisation behind, we skid back onto the M55 and embark on a 600km journey to Chita. After an hour on the road we begin to pass through the burning taiga. The word taiga originates from the Turkic language meaning "coniferous forests" and large areas of Siberia's taiga have been harvested for lumber since the collapse of the Soviet Union. Coal mining, logging, pollution and oil and gas development in the area all pose threats to the environment, with several major hydroelectric projects also planned. On either side of the road, charred trees smoulder like burnt matchsticks and flames leap sporadically into the air from patches of green forest. It feels like the world is on fire. We watch a roaring inferno attack an area close to the road and hear wood crack as a tree collapses in flames. I keep my eyes peeled for Siberian firefighters. Known as Smoke Jumpers, they parachute out of fifty-year old turbo powered Mi-8 helicopters, and spend weeks battling to bring wildfires under control. They survive by hunting for food and eating raw fish.

Not one single car or truck passes by as we make our way through the burning forest, and I begin to feel slightly concerned for our safety. Si reminds me of the words of the mighty Genghis Khan, "If you're afraid - don't do it - if you're doing it - don't be afraid!" Rummaging through the glove box I dig out the SAS Survival Guide.

I flick to the section on fire. 'Listen to this, Si. It says here, "Do not drive through thick smoke."'

'Bit late for that, isn't it?'

'"If caught in a fire find a clear area."'

Si frowns. 'There aren't any clear areas.'

'Hmm, okay, forget about that one, too. "Turn on the headlights and stay in the car".'

Si quickly flicks the lights on full beam.

'"Close all of the windows, turn off the ventilation, and stay in your vehicle until the glass begins to melt".'

'What?'

'It also mentions the danger of the fuel tank exploding.'

Si gulps. 'We're going to die, aren't we?'

'It's highly possible. Although, if the wind does change and the windows melt before the fire passes over the car, there is always the final option of burying ourselves in the earth.'

'Don't be ridiculous.'

'It's true,' I smile, pointing at the page. 'It says here, "If there is no natural break or gully in which to shelter and the fire is too deep to run through, you may have to seek the protection of the earth itself."'

All of a sudden, a squirrel darts across the road in front of us. Si swerves to avoid it, but we feel a bump as it disappears under one of the back wheels.

I clench my teeth. 'Poor blighter, what are the chances

of that? You escape the forest fire by the fluff of your tail, and then you get mowed down by the only car for miles around.'

Si shakes his head. 'Life's a bitch. I mean, what's the point?'

'In being a squirrel?'

'No, in life, we're on this planet for a nanosecond and then we simply disappear into dust.'

'That's a little morbid, buddy.'

'No, Chris, it's a fact. I mean, how do you think you'll die?'

'I don't know. It's not really on my list of important thing's to think about.'

'It crosses everybody's mind at some point.'

'Well, I guess you'd hope of old age, but considering our current situation that's looking pretty unlikely right now.'

'I hope I have the opportunity to look death in the eyes,' Si smiles, as we flash by more burning trees. 'Have a moment to say to myself, "so this is how the story ends. Bring it on!"'

Escaping death with each mile, we drive through the burning forests for a further 200 miles. Protected by the road, we eventually return to civilization, well, civilization as in a cluster of tin-pot shacks and a roadside café. We decide to make a pit stop. A strange looking guy standing behind the counter welcomes us inside. Dressed in black from head-to-toe, his complexion is ghostly pale and he has deep blue eyes and long black eyelashes. His nose is huge like a toucan's beak. We smile and study the menu. The guy speaks English and he seems keen to make conversation. I'm intrigued to learn he is from Armenia. Si asks him about the forest fires, but he just shrugs his shoulders. The mother, a slim woman with curly brown hair, emerges from a room at the back of the restaurant. A young boy follows close behind. I point to England on a map of the world pinned to the wall. They all smile and we exchange handshakes. The guy dressed in black seems pleased to meet two people from the British Isles and enthusiastically points to Armenia, a small country east of Turkey. He excitedly shows us a packet of cigarettes with the brand name "London" on the box. Si retrieves a couple of postcards of our hometown from his rucksack. The guy looks ecstatic and immediately pins them to the wall. I give the kid a couple of English coins, and he cups them in the palm of his hands like they are the most precious treasure known to man. Unable to enjoy a conversation of any depth, I feel annoyed with myself for having not learnt more Russian before leaving England. I'd love to ask them about their country and find out why they had ended up living all the way out here deep in Siberia. We discover the family moved to this region in 1991, and I wonder if they had been affected by the bloody Nagorno-Karabakh War, which had erupted between Armenia and Azerbaijan in the late 1980s. The mother cooks an incredible feast, and we leave the café feeling touched by their humble generosity.

Back on the road, the smoke slowly disappears and we continue to push east to Chita – the frontier of our journey. The sweet smell of Asia rolls across the dry, barren landscape. Si sings lyrics from his band days with 'The Blood Sucking Flower Fairies' and we play a few stupid games of eye spy. We nearly plough head on into a horse galloping towards us. Two kids hang on for dear life as they ride the beast bareback. They look so happy and free, and I admire the perfect simplicity of their lives. Si places a compass in the palm of his hand. We watch the needle settle and point east towards the horizon. For ten days now we have been travelling in the same direction. Each morning the sun rises in front of us in the east, it passes over our heads during the day and sets directly behind us in the west. We park up for the night at a rundown roadside café ten miles outside Chita. Like many of the places we've stopped at along our journey, it's a small wooden shack that's badly in need of repair. There's a plastic table and a couple of chairs on the porch outside the entrance, so we choose to sit outside and enjoy the remainder of the evening. While we try to work out what to eat, a large hulk of a man wearing a green vest top, who has dark stubble and tattoos on his arms, exits the café and limps over to our table. Si orders a couple of beers and some food. He returns with the beers that are as warm as bath water, but after a long hard day on the road it could be a bottle of the guy's piss and I'd probably still drink it. He has a red face and his eyes are puffed up. He looks like a heavy drinker, and you can tell by his body language that he was more than likely a soldier in the Russian army. His attitude is rock hard, and I get the distinct impression that if we stepped out of line he wouldn't hesitate to wring our necks like a couple of scrawny chickens. Si flashes him a 'please-don't-kill-us-we're-your-friends' kind of a smile. The guy throws two plates of burnt mush on the table and disappears inside the shack. A beautiful fair-haired woman carrying a metal bucket appears in the doorway.

Si's jaw hits the table. 'Holy Mother of Babylon,' he sings.

'Careful, she could be the guy's wife. If he sees you looking at her like that he might snap your skinny body in two.'

'That's what's missing from my life right now, a muse.'

I frown. 'As in a cul-de-sac?'

'No, you idiot, someone who inspires me, a reason to

breathe. Have you ever been in love, Chris?'

'Of course I have.'

'Who with?'

'Lucy. I think she's the only girl I've ever truly been in love with.'

'Hmm, that depends on how you define the word "love",' Si smirks, flicking a piece of charred sausage into his mouth.

I lean back in my chair and fold my arms. 'Love, a deep, tender, ineffable feeling of affection and solicitude toward a person, such as that arising from kinship, recognition of attractive qualities, or a sense of underlying oneness.'

'Who wrote that?'

'It's the definition of "love" in the English dictionary. I memorized it when I was a kid.'

'For what reason exactly?' Si asks looking concerned for my sanity.

'I guess I wanted to know what it meant.'

'And do you?'

'I think so. That feeling of losing your heart for the first time has a lasting effect. I haven't really been the same since. She was so beautiful. Those days were great fun. We would ride horses through the woods and make love in the wild meadows. It was all so innocent. I even bought her a plastic rose from a petrol station.'

'A plastic rose?'

'Uh-huh.'

'From a petrol station?'

'Yep.'

'Why?'

'I thought it would be romantic. You know, the rose would last forever.'

Si shakes his head and places his beer on the table.

'What a horrible thought, not romantic at all, buddy.'

The guy appears at the table with two more bottles of beer.

'Rooskee peeva, very good,' Si smiles, pointing at his bottle.

The guy shakes his head. 'Nyet, Rooskee peeva, Chech peeva,'

I glance at Si. 'Oh, I think he means Chechnyan peeva.'

'Nyet Chechnya!' the guy yells, slamming his fist down on the table. He marches back inside the café.

'You idiot, like he'd be a fan of beer from Chechnya!' Si snaps, darting paranoid glances around the porch. 'You do realize he's going to kill us now, don't you. He'll reappear in a second with a huge axe and chop us both up into little pieces.'

'Let's get the hell out of here!'

'Too late, quick, act normal, he's coming back.'

The guy returns with three beers and sits back down at the table. He doesn't have an axe and he appears to be quite chilled, which is good news. His beautiful wife appears in the doorway like a bright-eyed thorn. She begins to clear away our plates. I look over at Si, who distracts himself by glancing down at the road atlas. Breaking the silence, I show the guy our route from England, but he doesn't appear to be interested. Si points at Siberia and shivers. The guy nods his head firmly. He explains to us through hand gestures that during the winter months the roads are thick with snow, and he spends much of his time clearing it away from the house. It can reach the top of the door and the temperatures can plummet to a breathtaking -50°C. Si offers the guy an L&M cigarette, but he declines and pulls a packet of Russian cigarettes out of his pocket. The packet is red and made of cheap cardboard. They look like something our great grandfather might have smoked in the trenches during the battle of the Somme. Encouraging us to try one, I study the filterless cigarette between my fingers before accepting a light. Drawing hard, I choke on the harsh tasting tobacco and wipe away a tear from the corner of my eye. The guy laughs. He reaches over the table and pats me hard on the back.

'Angleeya, euro?' the guy asks, flicking ash onto the table.

'What's he say?'

Si shrugs. 'I think he's asking if we use euros in England.'

'Nyet, pound sterling,' I reply.

'Euro gutt, ruble nyet,' he laughs loudly.

'Da, euro gutt,' Si nods, whipping twenty euros out of his wallet.

Placing the note on the table in front of him, the guy looks surprised and studies it with intrigue. He then stubs his cigarette out on the floor and stumbles inside the café, returning seconds later with a book. He hands it to me and, despite the fact it's printed in Russian, I instantly recognize it as the Holy Bible. He offers it to us as a present along with an unopened packet of the harsh tasting cigarettes. Overwhelmed by his generosity, Si gets a little carried away and slides the twenty euro note across the table towards him.

'For you,' he smiles slurring his words a little.

The guy looks confused and points at the note and then at his chest, as if to say, "you're giving this money to me?" He stuffs the note into his trouser pocket and speedily clears away the table. Bidding us goodnight, he disappears inside the café and bolts the door shut behind him. The light goes out, and we sit in the dark clutching our bottles of beer. Feeling slightly uncomfortable to be sat on the guy's porch in the dark, we collect our possessions together and retire to the car.

The Final Frontier

Chita is a city deep in the arse end of nowhere. It's 6,200km from Moscow and is the last major stop before the Trans-Manchurian train line branches 100km east to China. Founded by the Cossacks in 1653, Chita boomed in the 20th Century with the completion of the mighty Trans-Siberian Railway and the new East Chinese Railway. Local Mongolic and Turkic tribes, along with various Chinese traders originally inhabited the region around Chita for several centuries before the Russians arrived.

According to our Russian friend in Yekaterinburg, this is where the Zilov Gap begins, a 650km section of harsh terrain in Central Siberia. Chris drives through the derelict streets of the city, and we glide past a black statue of three soldiers thrusting their rifles into the air. The usual drunks sit slumped at the side of the road and stare at us as we crawl along the main street lined with crumbling apartment buildings. We load up the Sierra with supplies, and pass a sinister ten-foot high inflatable gorilla that bobs from side to side above the roof of a concrete office building. We find a petrol station and fill up the car and our new reserve tank with fuel. I check the tyre pressure, fill the coolant reservoir with water and top up the engine with oil until the level is bang on the line. Everything appears to be in working order, and we feel content that we have done all we can before we attempt to drive into the unknown. Chris pulls out of the gas station and a police car immediately flags us down. One of the police officers looks to be of Chinese origin and he aggressively barks orders at us in Russian. We jump to attention and stand against the Sierra with our hands by our sides. Rummaging through the glove box the police officer retrieves the policeman's cap we had been given by the cops in Ivanovo. He shoots us both a look of suspicion. He then finds the half-empty bottle of vodka, provoking him to launch a verbal attack on us in the Russian language. We haven't a clue what he's saying and I watch salvia leap out of his mouth and land on my t-shirt. The officer holds the policeman's cap up to my face and, I assume he wants to know where we got it from. Pointing out the inscription on the bottle of vodka "from the Ivanovo police department", the police cop frowns. He then scrutinises our passports. Fortunately, we are saved from any further interrogation when a call comes through on his police radio. It appears to be urgent and throwing everything back at us, he leaps into his car and accelerates away at speed with flashing blue lights.

Feeling unnerved by the police shakedown, we leave Chita. After ten kilometers, the tarmac road is replaced by a dusty track that stretches to the horizon. Cutting across the wide-open plains, void of any trees, we can hear a low groan. At first we think it's the sound of the tyres on the unpaved highway, but it grows louder and we realise it's the wind howling across the vast landscape. To our right, we see a horse and cart thundering across the dry plains, with a huge dust cloud trailing behind and we watch in wonder at a scene from thousands of years ago. A silhouetted figure cracks a whip and two powerful horses, led by a pack of dogs, sprint at speed in the direction of Chita.

For several hours, Chris negotiates the deserted highway. Dark menacing clouds loom overhead. We reduce our speed to allow a Mongolian shepherd to cross the road in front of us with his flock. He carries a crooked staff and skilfully drives the dozens of curly horned sheep safely to the other side. They look unlike any sheep I have seen before, with thick woolly coats that protect them against the harsh Siberian winter. I look in awe at the old man's weather-beaten face. He has the complexion of tan boot leather and deep frown lines carved into his skin. He takes little notice of us and continues on his journey to the never-ending horizon. I can't help wondering where he is taking his flock, as there is literally no sign of life in any direction. According to our map the road ends here and the Zilov Gap begins; an 800km stretch of deep valleys, swamps and impenetrable forest that exists between Chita and Magdagachi. The construction of the Trans-Siberian Railway across this harsh landscape had been notoriously difficult, as it passed through thinly populated areas and impassable terrain. Approaching the frontier of our journey, the thought of driving this wild route in a sixteen-year-old saloon car begins to feel rather daunting.

We eventually arrive in the small frontier community of Chernyshevsk in Zabaykalsky Krai, which is located on both sides of the river Aleur. I take over the driving from Chris and we hit dense forest. After driving a painfully slow 70km section of road close to the Chinese border, we approach the small town of Mogocha; the administrative centre of the Mogochinsky District of Zabaykalsky Krai. Located at the confluence of the Mogocha and Amazar Rivers, this small town was founded in 1910, with the construction of the local section of the Trans-Siberian

Railway. From 1947 until 1953 Mogocha was also the site for the Klyuchevlag prison labour camp of the gulag system. The camp held up to 3,000 prisoners at any one time, and was mainly used as forced labour for molybdenum and gold mining. The town's remoteness combined with the harsh climatic conditions gave rise to the Soviet military slang expression "God created Sochi and Satan Mogocha". In Mogocha, wooden houses with blue shutters line the quiet streets next to half a dozen concrete apartment buildings. Spotting a small gas station we agree to seize what could be our last opportunity to top up with fuel. An old beige Lada pulls up beside us. A guy with scruffy white hair sticks his head out of the window and babbles something in Russian. He appears to have had a few drinks and his eyes are glazed and bloodshot. Collapsing out of his car he staggers over and peers through the passenger window. The guy hic-cups and narrows his small eyes. He mumbles something and laughs. His face is red from years of alcohol abuse and he has a bulbous nose. Leaning against the car door he points over his shoulder before pointing to us.

'Banya!' he slurs, saliva dribbling from his cracked bottom lip.

Chris frowns. 'What does that mean?'

'It's a Russian sauna and steam bath. Hang on. I think he wants us to join him for a sauna.'

'I don't think so, amigo,' Chris mumbles, screwing up his face.

The guy begins to laugh hysterically. Despite being in desperate need of a wash we politely decline his offer. He shuffles sideways and points at a grotty concrete tower block a few hundred metres away, and begins to flick a finger repeatedly against his throat. He appears to be inviting us to join him for a drink. Not wishing to offend the poor guy, I nod and smile and indicate to him that we're in a hurry. It turns out this is a wise decision, as he starts behaving strangely and proceeds tapping his wrist and simulates jacking-up with a hypodermic needle. I slowly roll the car forward. The guy lets go of the door and stumbles back to his Lada. Swinging the Sierra over to a couple of ancient petrol pumps, we top up the tank with 92 octane. A brand new Toyota pulls up on the other side of the pump and a tall Russian guy steps out and smiles. His mouth is filled with sparkling gold teeth. Tucking his smart polo shirt into his jeans, he greets us over the roof of the car. We try to ask him about the road ahead, but he fails to understand our sign language and shrugs his shoulders.

Leaving town, we continue for two hours along a bumpy road without seeing a single vehicle. Feeling vulnerable in the remote wilderness we park for the night behind a large abandoned Volvo digger. There really is no turning back now. Devouring a couple of tins of Black Sea sardines with a loaf of bread, Chris proceeds to scare the living daylights out of me with statistics about how far we have travelled and how far we still have to go. We are above China now and have passed through a staggering eight time zones. We are closer to Tokyo than Moscow and nearer to Seattle than London. Vladivostok is still over 3,000km away, which leaves us wondering what on earth lies in between?

* * *

At first light we drive for an hour and cross into Amur Oblast. Discovering the route ahead is blocked, a handmade wooden sign with an arrow pointing to the left diverts us down a narrow unpaved track leading into the dark forest. We have absolutely no idea where we are going. Hopefully the diversion will lead us up and around the road works and back onto the main road under construction. Si insists we play it safe and park up until we see another vehicle, that way we'll know for sure that we're heading in the right direction for Vladivostok. We wait for what feels like an eternity. I pace around and urinate at the roadside. It begins to feel like we are the last humans on the planet. Our morale deteriorates with each passing hour. Si dives into the back of the Sierra and immediately begins snoring. Despite Siberia accounting for 77% of Russia's vast territory, it has a relatively small population of just 40 million people. With the majority of the regions inhabitants living in the cities that have grown up along the Trans-Siberian railway line, it's insane to think that if they were evenly distributed across Siberia there would only be three individuals per square kilometre. Imaging the vast forests that fan out infront of me for thousands of miles, I feel suddenly very small and insignificant. The entire population of planet Earth could spontaneously combust and these forests would have barely even known we existed.

I collapse behind the wheel and drum a tune on the dashboard. With little to do except sit back and question my existence, I begin to think about home. Have we lost our minds? What are we trying to prove? We could get seriously lost out here, or kidnapped by a wild man never to be seen again. Are our lives really so terrible that we feel the need to confront danger in order to feel like we have achieved? I begin to wonder if maybe our road trips are just an excuse to escape the mundane world of the nine to five. Si was happy in London when he was with Emily. Have I led him astray? As a student in London I had watched people rushing around, jostling for position.

Everyone appeared to need to justify their place in the world. Money and a cool sounding job title appeared to be the motivator, but isn't it futile to chase success without first questioning why?

After six hours, I wake up with a cricked neck to the sound of a car door slamming shut. Si leaps into the front passenger seat. In an attempt to keep us both entertained, he begins to sing lyrics from his old band days with 'The Blood Sucking Flower Fairies'.

"I thought you were mine, the crack in the sink, drowning in the dirt.
You looked to the sky, salvation dead, just shit in your eye.
She, she's got time. She's got the time...
She, she's got time, to change her own mind.
I want to rub shoulders with the bourgeoisie...
I want to be single I want to be free.
I want to find culture and try to understand,
I guess I want to be in a rock 'n' roll band!"

I cast Si a look of irritation.

"...It took time to discover, that you weren't like any other.
Did you think you could make me suffer?
Well I'll tell you girl I can find another.
Well I'll tell you girl I can find another-er..."

'...Give it a rest, will you!' I yell in despair, holding my head in my hands.
'Chill out, I'm a rock god.'
'No, Si, you're not a rock god, you're an ageing hippie, who thinks he's a...hey, what's that?'

Snatching the binoculars off the dashboard I leap out of the Sierra.

'What is it?' Si asks, squinting into the bright sunlight.

'I think it's a car.'

'Are you sure?'

'I can see a dust cloud. It is! It's a car!'

We can see the vehicle clearly now as it thunders towards us. More cars appear over the horizon – two, four, five. Putting on our headlights for fear of them not seeing us, we sound our horn as a Toyota saloon and a Mitsubishi estate race by. The cars all toot their horns and flash their lights as an enormous cloud of dust fills the air.

'They're all Japanese vehicles,' Si laughs with excitement. 'Maybe they've driven here from Vladivostok!'

'Yeah, look, they haven't got registration plates.'

Si reaches through the driver's side window and sounds the horn, and we watch as a second convoy speeds past. Some of the drivers are wearing white gloves, and others are stripped to the waist or wearing shades. All of the brand new cars have protective covers over their headlights and masking tape wrapped around their bumpers. As the dust settles we head off in the opposite direction, and pass more cars travelling in convoy along the dirt track. We see brand new Toyota saloons and Mitsubishi estates with tyre blowouts, and watch the drivers change the wheels at great speed like F1 mechanics in the pit lanes. From out of nowhere, a huge orange overland truck charges up behind us and virtually kisses our rear bumper. The massive grill on the front of the truck fills the rear view mirror as it tries desperately to overtake. The driver swerves around our back end, but quickly pulls in when another convoy of cars fly past in the opposite direction. The truck tries again, this time managing to pull up alongside us. I battle to control the Sierra, but I'm forced to slam on the brakes. I catch a glimpse of the registration plate and realise they're German. Despite feeling angry about their frantic manoeuvre, we're excited to see a fellow pioneer on the road. Si waves out of the sunroof. The enormous truck ignores us and accelerates away. Tyre marks from the German's truck are clearly visible in the dust, and I begin to feel annoyed by the fact that we're trailing behind in their shadow. The sensation of the open road is scarred by their presence, and I find it difficult to relax. We approach a flatbed truck that's carrying two new Japanese cars on the back. The driver skilfully weaves around an enormous crater in the road. Potholes are our main concern here, and every few metres the exhaust pipe is dragged along the earth. We cringe with every scrape, but it doesn't seem to make any difference how slow we drive or how hard we try to avoid the potholes, the Sierra is just too low to the ground. With no option, other than to turn around and head back to Chita, we're forced to grit our teeth and hope for the best as we push deeper and deeper into the thick forest. We're eventually brought to a halt by a deep river, a deep river without a bridge.

'I hope you've brought your arm bands?' I smile, revving the engine.

'You're not seriously going to drive through that, are you?'

'Of course I am. What else are we going to do, wait for the water to evaporate?'

'Shouldn't we check to see how deep it is first?'

'It can't be that deep.'

Si frowns. 'How do you know?'

'I don't…'

Slamming my foot down on the accelerator pedal, the

front wheels spin as the Sierra speeds towards the river.

'Hold onto your bollocks, hippie boy!'

'Holy shit!' Si yells, sinking his fingernails into the dashboard.

With a gigantic splash the car nosedives into the river. The water hits the window screen with a loud thud and sprays into the air. With adrenaline pumping through our veins, the car flies out onto the other side of the bank.

After sometime we find ourselves on a relatively flat stretch of road that carries us beneath a bridge supporting the Trans-Siberian train line. Following the train tracks for a few miles, we stumble across a pretty house and a café at a bend in the road. We walk through a small yellow gate into a well kept garden, and sit down on a wooden picnic bench. A woman of Chinese origin stands in the doorway to the house and rocks a baby in her arms. On the far side of the garden, a man wearing a camouflage jacket drives a wooden post into the ground with a sledgehammer.

'Are you sure this is a café?' Si whispers, darting glances around the garden.

The woman calls over to the guy building the fence. He drops his sledgehammer to the ground and marches over to us. He sweats profusely and dusts himself down. With dark features and thick stubble, he looks more Italian than Russian. We order two bowls of borshch and some coffee. He smiles and disappears into the house. After a hearty lunch of borsch and a plate of fried chicken noodles, the man walks over and points at our road map. He seems interested to know where we are from. Si points to England and the man points to Azerbaijan.

'Caspian Sea,' I beam.

The man nods vigorously. 'Da, Caspian.'

He points past the house towards the train tracks.

'Chita?' he grins.

Si frowns. 'Chita?'

The guy points to us both. 'Chita?'

'No, no,' Si replies. 'Vladivostok.'

He looks surprised and encourages us to follow him across the garden. He swings open the garden gate and waves us over. We march across the dirt road and wade through knee length grass to the railway tracks. Two train lines run parallel to each other, one heading to Moscow and the other to Vladivostok. With caution we stand on the wooden sleepers. The guy points up the line towards the horizon.

'Vladivostok,' he smiles.

The train tracks stretch out into the distance, and I look with excitement in the direction of a city we long to see. I savour this incredible opportunity to stand with my feet on the legendary Trans-Siberian Railway line. Returning to the café, we pay the bill and shake the guy by the hand. We head over to the Sierra and, just as I'm about to jump inside, I hear the roaring sound of an approaching train.

'It's the Trans-Siberian!' Si yells.

We run as fast as we can through the long grass and stand at the side of the tracks. The guy from the café runs to the garden gate and points in its direction.

'Vladivostok!' he cries.

The train grows bigger and bigger until it thunders past us at great speed, whipping Si's hair across his face. We jump in the air and dance around as each carriage rattles by one by one. A western guy with long hair peers out of the window. We think he might be a tourist, so we wave madly at him.

'We're from England!' I shout.

The guy cranes his neck as he zips past. Out of breath, we watch the last carriage disappear into the distance.

* * *

Waving farewell to our friend from Azerbaijan and his cute family, Chris sparks up the engine and we return to the forest. The road becomes increasingly narrow and steep and we're forced to zigzag from side to side in order to manoeuvre the Sierra over craters in the road that are literally the size of the car. This tends to be a disruption for the driver's of the cars from Vladivostok, our guardian angels, who are forced to wait for us to pass by. It occurs to me that we must be the first people to cause a traffic jam in deepest Siberia. From the state of the road, it's clear this track has been heavily used for quite some time. The deep craters in the earth are worn away more steeply on the far side, making it nearly impossible for us to haul the Sierra out the other side without scraping the exhaust pipe along the ground. This becomes a major problem, and we're unable to drive for more than a few metres without getting stuck. Forced to drive into one particularly deep crater, Chris revs the engine and accelerates up the steep side. We hear a loud crunch. Jumping out, we run around to the rear and inspect the damage. The join in the middle of the exhaust pipe has been completely torn apart and it is now lying in two pieces below the car. Lying on the dry earth, we somehow manage to slot them back together and apply exhaust paste and wrap kitchen foil and wire around the seal for extra strength. Drenched in sweat and oil, it takes five hours for us to reach the summit of this treacherous climb, covering a total distance of six miles. I gulp down a litre of water. Chris cuts the engine and leans back in his seat. He looks physically and mentally drained. On a nearby tree, I notice there are colourful pieces of ribbon and strips of plastic tied to the branches. They look like Christmas decorations and, examining them closer, we notice one or two have messages scribbled on them in Russian.

'This must be the halfway point,' Chris smiles. 'Everyone who has reached the top has tied something to the tree.'

'I've read about this, they're called wishing trees. It's similar to prayer flags of Tibetan Buddhism, the religion of most Buryats.'

'Wishing trees, how cool. We should make a wish.'

I frown 'What shall we wish for?'

Chris's eyes widen and a big smile appears across his face. 'A car full of sexy chicks to rock up.'

'Something realistic.'

'Okay, how about world peace.'

'I said something realistic.'

'A four day working week?'

'Not bad.'

'A safe journey to Vladivostok?'

'Perfect!'

Grabbing a carrier bag, Chris cuts off one of the handles with a blunt penknife and flattens it out on the hood. He picks up the marker pen and writes "UK to Vladivostok: Raven Brothers: June 2003". He ties it firmly to the branches of the tree. We stand back and admire our handy work. I turn away and look down the other side of the hill. Now all we have to do is get down.

Reaching a remote village at the bottom of the hill, a couple of guardian angels stand by their vehicles and prepare for the climb. You can tell by the worried expression across their faces that this section of the road is notorious and, having barely survived it ourselves, we throw them a wave and wish them luck. We drive past a derelict building and see three grubby little faces appear over the rubble. These hostile savages, who look about five or six-years-old, are stripped to the waist and scramble rat-like towards the car. I wave at them out of the window, but they respond by hurling pieces of brick and concrete at us. One jagged piece of slate scuffs across the hood and Chris sounds the horn and accelerates away. The village is perfectly simple, and was most probably locked away from the outside world until now. It feels like we've travelled back in time a hundred years, and I wonder what they make of all these vehicles descending on their world and ruining their tranquillity. An old man staggers out of his garden gate and flags us down. He grips onto the side of the car and rants and rages at us. Chris attempts to ask him for directions to Vladivostok, but he looks confused, quite understandably really, as Vladivostok is still approximately two thousand miles away. He won't let go of the door and continues to shout at us as we try to explain to him that we can't speak Russian. Chris points to England on the map, and this is all too much for a man who has more than likely spent his entire life in the remote wilderness. He looks about eighty years old, and was most probably a young boy of about ten when the Gulags (labour camps) were put into operation. As part of Stalin's grand plan to turn the USSR into an industrial power in 1929, he forced collectivisation of agriculture with the aim of getting peasants to fulfil production quotas, which would feed the growing cities and provide food exports to pay for imported heavy machinery. Farmers who resisted were either killed or deported to labour camps in their millions. Looking into his pale grey eyes, I wonder what stories he has to tell about that time. He seems upset by this sudden invasion to his world. Finally losing his grip on the door, he throws up his hands in despair. I feel guilty as we pull away, but I console myself with the thought that before long, in seven or eight years or so, the Amur highway will be complete and this village will be returned to the wilderness once more. After an hour, we begin to see large Volvo diggers and find ourselves back on the highway under construction. We cruise at 20mph along a stony section of the road until it gets dark. Pulling up close to the impenetrable forest, we pass out after nearly sixteen hours on the road.

In the early hours of the morning, Chris crawls under the Sierra and patches up the torn kitchen foil wrapped around the exhaust system. He does a fantastic job and putting some air in the tyres with the squeaky foot pump, we feel confident to head back on the road. We drive through the morning until we reach a stretch of the highway that is undergoing major construction. Enormous diggers shovel tons of earth and Volvo dumper trucks tower above the Sierra, as they transport rocks and stones along never ending stretches of the highway. We crawl beneath their huge wheels and weave along tracks that tail off into deep canyons. We battle against the road works from dawn until dusk, at an average speed of approximately 5mph. Sections of the road force us to climb steep hills at a frightening angle of 45 degrees, and we approach each turn cautiously for fear of colliding with a digger or one of the many guardian angels travelling in the opposite direction. Reversing and shunting through freshly laid gravel, we cautiously manoeuvre the Sierra along the edge of crumbling earth banks and weave around enormous boulders. At one point we nearly tip sideways down a twenty foot drop. It takes incredible concentration and, driving over sharp rocks and smashing the bumper into the ground, we curse out of anger and laugh out of insanity with every knock and scrape. Desperately trying to stay sane, we head slowly towards the never-ending horizon.

Spending a second night on the Amur highway, we pass through the small outback town of "Never" around noon. The place feels like a city after more than three days in the wilderness. The Sierra looks like a wreck. The front bumper hangs close to the ground and is held in place by little more than some electrical tape and a fist full of rubber bands. The bodywork is caked in mud and exhaust fumes leak from under the car. To make matters worse there appears to be something wrong with the starter motor, because when we turn off the ignition the car rattles and shakes for about thirty seconds before the engine stalls. We fill up with petrol, grab more supplies from a small shop and try to find our way out of the town. We soon become lost and find ourselves heading up an asphalt track, which Chris thinks might be the M56 to Yakutsk and Magadan. In 1932, Stalin sent thousands of prisoners to Magadan to build docks and piers, so they could transport gold found in the Kolyma region. It became a major marshalling point for the prisoners, who were sent there to work in the mines. Being sent to Magadan was a death sentence. Of over the estimated 20 million people who were shot, starved, beaten, tortured or worked to death in Stalin's Gulag camps, an estimated one fifth died in camps around the Kolyma region. The road to Magadan is even called the Road of Bones because of the thousands of prisoners who died building it.

Through a haze of dust we see an orange truck heading towards us. It's the Germans! We flash our lights and they pull over on the opposite side of the road. I turn off the ignition, but the engine continues to rattle and shake vigorously before cutting out. We meet the driver at the front of his massive overland truck. He looks over at the Sierra and seems amused by our completely impractical choice of vehicle. He's a fairly young chap in his early thirties, with rectangular metal-framed glasses. A sulky looking woman with her arms folded is sat high up in the passenger seat and glares down at us.

'Your destination is Vladivostok?' the German guy asks.

'Yes, Vladivostok here we come,' I smile.

'We travel there also.'

'Where are you from in Germany?' Chris asks.

'We live in Munich.' He looks over at the Sierra and shakes his head. 'Your car will not make it, I think.'

I nod. 'You could be right. It is starting to fall apart.'

'You sleep in this vehicle?'

'I'm afraid so, it's really uncomfortable,' Chris laughs, arching his back.

'You have GPS?'

'No GPS, but we've got a really good road atlas we bought in St Petersburg,' I smile.

Chris seizes the opportunity to ask for directions. 'Is this the road to Magadan?'

The guy looks embarrassed. 'Ya, we made the wrong turn.' He looks over his shoulder at the woman sat in the truck. '…okay, so I made the wrong turn.' He shakes his head and changes the subject. 'It seems we are the first Europeans to drive this road.'

'How do you know?'

'A mechanic in Irkutsk told us it was not possible last summer. We are the first westerners to drive on this new road to Vladivostok.' He begins to slowly back away. 'We are the first.'

'How long have you been on the road?' I ask.

He swings open the driver's door. 'We left Bavaria one

month ago. We plan to ship our vehicle from Vladivostok to Australia.'

'What a fantastic adventure!'

I consider inviting them to join us for a cup of tea, but he seems in a hurry to leave. Scrambling aboard the truck he strikes the engine and, bidding us farewell, he accelerates away at great speed. We stand in the middle of the road, confused by their hasty departure.

Chris frowns. 'Was it something we said?'

'Quick, get in the car.'

'Why?'

I slide across the hood. 'It looks like the race is on!'

The Amur Hellway

'Faster!' Si yells, as I whack the Sierra into third gear.

The windows are down, the sunroof is open and Si's crazy hair dances in the wind. We skid back onto the main road under construction and literally fly through the air, hitting pothole after pothole like they're little more than irritating obstacles in our path. Determined to catch up with the Germans we happily risk destroying the car. Less than an hour ago we were driving on this road at 5mph, now it's more like 50mph. The risk of the suspension collapsing seems irrelevant to us at this moment in time.

Si turns to me with a smile. 'I can see their truck up ahead. We're gaining on them. Vladivostok will be ours.'

Without warning, one of the back tyres explodes and the Sierra swerves sharply to the left and then to the right before sliding across the highway and crashing sideways into a huge pile of gravel. We jump out of the car and inspect the damage. It's not good. The tyre is completely shredded and there's a nasty dent in the driver's door.

'Idiots!' Si yells, pacing up and down. 'What are we going to do now?'

'Let's not panic. At least we've got two spares.'

'They're in a right state. One has got a six inch nail buried in it and the other is buckled beyond repair.'

'Yes, but they still work. They still roll.'

We dive into the trunk and forage for the jack and one of the spare wheels. Si uses the lug wrench to loosen the wheel nuts, but tugging at the wheel it appears to be welded on tight.

'The damn thing is stuck,' he sighs.

'Let me have a go.'

I grab hold of the wheel and use a foot and my entire body weight, but to no avail. A sharp pain shoots down my left arm, which causes me to release my grip and fall backwards onto the gravel. I shake the dust out of my hair and we gradually come to the conclusion that we're going to die out here in the remote wilderness. All of a sudden, a huge Volvo dumper truck carrying a cargo of rubble skids to a halt beside us. A muscular guy with a bare chest leaps out of the driver's cab and swaggers over. He looks down at the shredded tyre.

Si grabs the phrasebook and flicks to a page. 'Shina prakolata,' he beams. 'I have a puncture.'

The guy nods and using his considerable strength he tries to pull it off. Springing to his feet, he walks over to his truck and returns with a crowbar. After a few attempts, he manages to wrench it free. We shake him firmly by the hand and thank him in Russian. The guy seems pleased to have been of some assistance. Communicating with him through the phrasebook, we discover he has just finished a month working on the Amur highway and that he is due to return home to Magdagachi tomorrow. Thrusting his hips backwards and forwards, he dry humps the car and informs us with a smile that he is going to have lots of sex with his girlfriend. We laugh and congratulate him with high fives. He grabs his crotch and pulls a face before scrambling aboard his truck. Waving a hand in the air, he tears off down the road like the world is about to explode.

Changing the wheel with relative ease, we both agree that if we are going to successfully make it to Vladivostok we need to retire from the race and travel at a more relaxed pace. Returning to road, Si drives and we pass enormous concrete flyovers that are under construction and cross fast flowing rivers and wide canyons. Workmen wearing yellow hard hats perspire in the heat of the day, as they shift millions of tons of earth. We follow a dirt track that skims alongside a line of huge concrete pillars that sprout out of the ground like bizarre Neolithic monuments. The Amur highway that will run over the top hasn't even been built yet, and we feel privileged to witness this incredible feat of engineering with our very own eyes. In a couple of years, this dirt road we are driving on will be reclaimed by the forest and returned to the wilderness once more.

A bright red sun stirs me from my sleep. Its early morning and we're parked on an elevated mud bank overlooking the vast green forest. Si drives for an hour before we stumble across a small wooden makeshift shed. An old man with a grey beard and liquid green eyes invites us to sit down. He cooks a hearty breakfast of scrambled eggs and fried dough covered in sugar, and fixes us a strong black coffee. Enjoying the experience of eating breakfast at a temporary café located deep in the Siberian wilderness, we're reminded once more of the adaptability of humans who appear capable of surviving in the most hostile environments. Paying the old chap a few rubles for the fantastic morning feast, we take the opportunity to splash our faces and wash the dust out of our hair in a nearby river. Back on the road, we see a large camp that houses the hundreds of men working on this remote stretch of the highway. Huge trucks and diggers line up outside a long row of portacabins. A group of sun-tanned guys wearing hard hats stand at the roadside and smoke cigarettes. One of the workmen flags us down. I grab the phrasebook and hand it to him. He flicks through the pages, but with a shrug of the shoulders he hands it back. The guy then points to his fellow workers and then up the highway. He appears to be asking for a lift, but a lift to where? On these road conditions driving 5mph for 50km could take two days. I can smell booze on his breath and he peers inside the car and looks around before walking back to the group of workmen. They all look over and laugh. Reluctant to risk putting any more pressure on the already straining suspension and threadbare tyres, Si speeds away. Well, at least he tries. The four drunken construction workers chase after us. They quit after a hundred metres and watch as we slowly crawl off into the distance.

Pumping air into the tyre with the six inch nail stuck inside, Si continues to drive east. We pause when we see a handmade sign with a drawing of a petrol pump painted on it. The arrow points down a dirt track that tails off into the forest. The idea of leaving the main highway unnecessarily seems completely insane. Unsure when the next opportunity to refuel will be, we agree it's worth the risk. We make our way cautiously through the forest for approximately 30km. The thought of breaking down out here makes me feel physically sick, because the chances of anyone passing by are incredibly slim. At least if we get stuck on the Amur highway there's a chance someone will come to our aid within a few hours, but if it happens out here we'll have to walk back to the main highway and persuade someone to come to our rescue. We eventually spot a cluster of wooden houses on the far side of a river. Si draws to a halt in front of a rickety wooden bridge.

He shakes his head. 'There's no way we're driving across that.'

'Of course we are.'

'Have you lost your mind?'

'What's the big deal?'

'The bridge isn't strong enough to support the weight of a car.'

'If it can support a horse and cart, surely it can support a car.'

'Let's find somewhere else to get fuel.'

I laugh. 'There isn't anywhere else.'

'What about the reserves?'

'We've already used one tank.'

'So, let's use the other one, then?'

'Si, that's for emergencies.'

'This is an emergency!'

'We need reserves. We have to get more.' I step onto the rotten bridge and peer over the edge. 'It'll be fine.'

'How can we be sure it won't collapse?'

'There's a petrol station in the village on the other side. Cars must cross this bridge all of the time.'

Si frowns. 'What cars? There aren't any cars!'

I ignore him and leap behind the wheel. Flicking down my sunglasses I slowly inch forward. Si gives in and helps me line up the front wheels with the wooden planks. There's a gap running down the middle of the bridge and I can see the rushing water below. As the front tyres mount the wooden slats they creek under the weight of the Sierra. To my right there is a hole about a foot wide. I cautiously manoeuvre around it and I can feel my heart pounding inside my chest. The bridge sways a little and continues to creek, but thankfully we make it safely across to the other side. We pass the deserted wooden shacks on the opposite bank and see a rusty sign with the symbol for a petrol pump. A huge pile of coal has been dumped in front of a house, obstructing the view outside their window. There doesn't appear to be anyone around, and I presume the inhabitants are all at work in the quarries or mines that surround this area. We pass under a large railway bridge and approach a small mining community. Following a road made of coal we reach a yard in the shadow of the railway line. I pull up beside an antique petrol pump, and we look in awe at an old rusty steam engine deteriorating in the long grass. While Si sorts out the petrol, I stretch my legs and decide to check out this incredible relic of Russia's past. It's in serious need of restoration, but with a slap of paint it would look great in a museum. In an instant, I see something in the corner of my eye. I turn and look in terror as an enormous black dog runs towards me across the yard. I'm paralyzed with fear from the eyes down and unable to cry for help. The beast leaps at my throat, but luckily the chain around its neck goes taught and it's pulled violently back. This only torments the dog more, causing it to growl savagely and foam at the mouth. It's the size of a bear and looks like a Caucasian Shepherd dog; a breed commonly used in the mountains of southern Russia for hunting bears and wolves. Its piercing bark penetrates my eardrums and its sharp three inch long teeth drip saliva. I race back to the Sierra, and the kid filling our fuel tank appears to find my near death experience rather amusing. Wearing overalls, he has bright orange hair and a splatter of freckles across the bridge of his nose. With the appearance of a Scotsman, he looks strangely out of place in a region of Siberia that is only fifty kilometres from the Chinese border. We wave farewell to the carrot-topped kid, and return cautiously across the bridge to the safety of the highway. We reach a section of the road that is fully asphalt and completely pothole-free. Blinking in disbelief, we approach a brand new road sign. It's the first one we've seen on the Amur highway, and we cheer loudly and dance around it in wild celebration. It's an incredible sight to see, particularly as it informs us that we are now only 965km from Khabarovsk in the Far East of Siberia and less than 2,000km from Vladivostok.

The Executioner

Dazzled by a car's headlights, I massage my tired eyes. Blinking, I look over at Chris who sits glazed in the passenger seat next to me. It's deeply surreal to be back on a tarmac highway after being in the remote wilderness for so long. To my left, I see an orange glow of a city and I feel a strange combination of relief and anxiousness at the sight of civilization. I had grown used to the imposing wilderness, despite our fears of becoming stranded. Our focus had been to survive the notorious road under construction, and making it to the other side we have instantly been zapped back to reality; into a world without the problems of crossing rivers, bridges and negotiating hazardous terrain.

A white figure suddenly flashes across my field of vision. 'Wow, did you see that?'

Chris jumps in his seat and looks around. 'What?'

'Something crossed the road. I think it was a person. Shit, I don't feel good. I'm going to pull over.'

I begin to feel nauseous and stumble out of the car. I spin around in circles and clutch my forehead.

'Si, are you okay?'

'Head rush.'

I lie down on the tarmac and look up at the stars. The

clear night sky swirls above my head. I feel like I've just stepped off a roller coaster or knocked back a bottle of tequila.'

'Maybe it's the exhaust fumes?' Chris sighs, shining a torch under the car.

I sit up and take a deep breathe. Climbing unsteadily to my feet, I feel as high as a kite. The ground swells like the ocean beneath me. I stumble over to the Sierra and begin to tear large chunks out of an incredibly dry loaf of bread. I take a swig of water, but it hits my stomach with a bang and I immediately projectile vomit all over the highway. Chris slaps me hard around the face, which does little more than numb my cheek.

'What the fuck?'

'Si, stay calm, buddy boy!'

'I am calm!' I shout, tearing another huge chunk out of the bread.

Chris slaps me around the face again, this time numbing the other cheek.

'Stop doing that!'

'You have to stay awake! We've poisoned ourselves!'

I squat down and try to clear my vision. I rub my cheek and continue to devour the loaf of bread.

'There's no way we're carrying on,' Chris demands, shaking his head. 'We're not risking it. Now we've picked up speed carbon monoxide is leaking from the exhaust into the car. It's too dangerous!'

Afraid to sleep, I lie outstretched across the backseat and moan feverishly. Sometime in the early hours, a car skids into the lay-by and a group of people begin setting off fireworks. It appears to be a wedding party. I glance at the clock; it's two o'clock in the morning. Burying my head inside my sleeping bag I pray for morning to arrive.

I'm disturbed from a deep sleep by an unfamiliar scraping sound. My head begins to pound at the temple again like someone has just smacked me over the head with the squeaky foot pump. I find the strength to investigate and squat down on my hands and knees and watch Chris patch up the exhaust.

'I thought you said it was road trip was over?'

Chris wriggles from beneath the car and dusts himself down. 'We have to push on. We're so close.'

'But what about the carbon monoxide?'

'We'll just have to drive with all of the windows down.'

With the exhaust pipe tightly wrapped in kitchen foil and the windows and sunroof fully open, we hit the open road. Empty crisp packets fly around inside the car as the temperature outside begins to soar. We pass a turn off for the town of Svobodny on the P468 and cross over the Zeya River, where we stop at a trucker's café near to the village of Novobureyskiy in Amurskaya Oblast. Opening the creaky door, we enter the small portacabin and grab a seat at a table by the window. It's incredibly hot inside, and a plague of flies buzz angrily behind the wire mesh. Chris peers down at the coffee stained menu. A large woman wearing a floral print apron, who looks like she has literally just given birth behind the counter, approaches our table and takes our order. An overweight guy is sat at a table behind and devours a plate of mashed potatoes and fried eggs. He looks like a mafia Godfather, with his big yellow tinted shades and a stomach that swells beneath his white vest. He looks over at us and says something to the waitress in a gravely voice. She shrugs her shoulders and he roars with laughter. I try to avoid eye contact with him, but I find it difficult not to stare. Chris looks deeply uncomfortable and wipes sweat from his forehead. We quickly lose our appetites and decide to make a hasty retreat while we still have kneecaps.

Crossing over the Bureya River, we arrive in the small village of Novobureyskiy and drive on a long straight road that cuts through the vast coniferous forests of the Siberian taiga. China, the third largest country by area in the world after Canada and Russia, is now only 15km away. The M58 bears to the left and we skim through the gold mining village of Obluchye. Weaving around yet another isolated Soviet village, with its ghostly feel and old wooden houses, we continue on towards the city of Birobidzhan. Technically, Israel is not the only official Jewish homeland in the world. Hidden away out here in Siberia, on the border with China and nearly 8,500km from Moscow, is the Jewish Autonomous region of Birobidzhan. It was founded in 1928, twenty years before the establishment of Israel, and was the result of Lenin's nationality policy.

Checking out a newly built roadside café on the edge of town, we head inside and discover a kid's party is in full swing. The energetic rug rats run wild around the café and weave around the tables and chairs to really loud music. A teenager, who is wearing a Jewish kippah, a brimless skullcap, walks over and sparks up a conversation. He reveals in perfect English that he has many online friends from the UK. We discover Levi's father is a successful entrepreneur, who owns many hotels and restaurants in the area. Chris asks him what life is like living out here in the Far East, and he reveals that things are changing fast. With Russia opening up and China set to boom, the people of the region are keen to profit.

'My father says it is our turn to have some fun,' Levi smiles. 'There are big opportunities for us now in Siberia.'

Curious to hear Levi talking openly about politics, he

also informs us how the people living in this region do not like to be dictated to by Moscow.

'The Russian Far East is like a different country,' Levi nods. 'We are completely cut off from the rest of Russia.'

The importance of Putin building a road linking Europe with Asia seems suddenly crystal clear. The completion of the Amur highway would not only increase trade, but it would also help unify this colossal country. Levi gets dragged onto the dancefloor, so we wave goodbye to the party and push on with our journey. We reach the wide Amur River and cross a spectacular bridge that carries us directly into the heart of Khabarovsk. From the Tungusic people many centuries ago to the Manchu Qing Dynasty, this large city in the Russian Far East has had a very colourful past. Today, with its Mediterranean resort feel and tree-lined streets, Japanese cars, museums, sushi restaurants and hockey heroes, Khabarovsk is definitely a Trans-Siberian stopover. Booming from the pharmaceutical industry, iron processing, steel milling and petroleum refining, the city was named in honour of pioneer Erofey Khabarov and it was here after the defeat of Japan, where the War Crime Trials took place after World War II.

Staying true to our plan, we resist the temptations of Khabarovsk and join the Ussuri highway heading south to Vladivostok on the Sea of Japan. This is the last stretch of our epic journey, with only 800km to travel before we reach our final destination. Hugging the Chinese border and China's northeast Heilongjiang Province, we cross the Khor River, which is one of the largest rivers of the west Sikhote-Alin. The Khor river banks have for centuries been home to the Udegeis, the native population of this region. The Udege are mainly engaged in hunting, fishing and ginseng picking and their religious beliefs include animism, animal worship and shamanism. We skim past the small town of Vyazemsky on the Trans-Siberian Railway line before entering the beautiful and wild Primorski krai. This Maritime Province has a warmer, wetter climate and, instead of the coniferous taiga, the well-watered land supports hardwood forests similar to those found in eastern China and the eastern United States. For centuries, this region was under the influence of the rulers of China and some of the native tribes paid tribute to the Chinese emperor before the area was ceded to Russia in 1860. Several native peoples, all related rather closely to the Ewenki in language and customs, lived in this area during the 17th Century. This beautiful wild region curves south along the Sea of Japan like a giant claw. It is home to the Sikhote-Alin mountain range, a subtropical zone rich in flora and fauna that flourishes unlike anywhere else on earth. In this spectacular territory in Russia's Far East, brown bear, lynx, reindeer and wolf cross paths with the Asiatic Black bear, the Siberian (Amur) tiger and the extremely rare Amur leopard. With poaching, logging, fires and development all posing a serious threat to these magnificent animals habitats, tragically there are only an estimated 30 Amur leopards and 400 Amur tigers left in the wild.

Continuing south to Vladivostok we stumble across a large pond. Within seconds, Chris is stripped down to his underpants and is swimming in the refreshing shallows. Following his lead, I jump off the bank and dunk my head under the water. Feeling instantly revitalised, I contemplate staying here for the remainder of the day, but I suddenly notice green slime sticking to my chest. Spoiling my fun, I swim to the bank and stagger out of the water like a slimy green swamp monster. Chris doesn't seem to mind the slime and continues to splash around in the water. Grabbing a razor, I examine my face in the reflection of the cracked wing mirror. My skin looks wind burnt and the lines around my eyes look more prominent after weeks of living on the road. Working up lather with a bar of soap in the frying pan, the blunt, slightly rusty razor scrapes across my patchy stubble as salty beads of sweat run into my eyes. If this isn't challenging enough, I'm attacked by a swarm of giant Siberian horseflies. They land on my face, pricking the skin with their spiky legs and buzz maliciously around my ears and nostrils. Spinning around, I swipe the air with irritation and resort to grabbing my towel and whipping the air. I hear Chris's screams from the water, and through blurry eyes I see him running out of the pond with a cloud of these flesh-eating insects buzzing above his head. We both hop around like Laurel and Hardy, desperately trying to pull on our shorts while frantically waving our arms above our heads. Diving into the Sierra we slam the doors shut, but the vicious insects dart through the open windows and sunroof and continue to launch their attack. Cursing and swatting the air, I reverse the car onto the highway. The majority of these savage insects abandon ship, but those crazy enough to stick around suffer a terrible fate at the hands of Chris "the executioner" and join the butterflies on the back parcel shelf.

* * *

Half-shaved and stripped to the waist, Si drives with bare feet along the highway as the last Siberian horsefly meets its fate. We stop for the night at a café close to the town of Dalnerechensk. A Chinese family mill around outside, and hungry as wolves we enter the canteen with its cold white washed walls. Pale faced Russian women wearing green aprons serve up food from large stainless steel containers. On a nearby table a woman of Chinese origin devours a steaming bowl of broth. She slurps noisily and shovels the food into her mouth at surprising speed. All of a sudden she begins to choke. Gasping for air, she clutches her throat and turns a terrifying shade of purple. The guy sat opposite leaps out of his seat and begins to perform the Heimlich Maneuver. As the woman gasps for what appears to be her final breath, the guy clutches her tighter around the waist and thrusts his hands hard into her stomach. Much to everyone's relief, a chicken bone shoots out of her mouth and skids across the table. They both collapse to the floor in a heap and the woman bursts into tears. With the drama over, our fellow diners return to eating their food and the women behind the counter continue with their work.

Finishing our basic meal of beef with mashed potatoes and carrots, we leave the café. Before settling down for the night, I go in search of a toilet, and find a neglected restroom at the back of the building. I flick on the light switch, which doesn't work, and enter the foul smelling room. The door slams shut behind me, and I blindly urinate in the direction of the toilet bowl before turning to the sink. I can just about see my face in the cracked mirror. I rinse my hands under the tap and reach for the door handle, but to my utter horror I discover there isn't one. Running my fingers frantically over the hole, where the handle should be, I desperately begin to scan every inch of the doorframe. I curse under my breath as panic grips hold of me. Feeling my heart beating violently inside my chest, I dart glances around this tiny toilet. Everywhere I look I can see the faint outline of the white ceramic tiles. The room begins to spin and I grip onto the wash basin and lower my head.

'Stay calm, Chris,' I whisper to myself.

Regaining my composure, my pulse is sent racing out of control again when it occurs to me that no one knows where I am. The café is closed and Si is most probably fast asleep. Being trapped in a small space is one of my worst fears. You're helpless, confined between four walls, which at this moment in time appear to be closing in on me. I take a deep breath and notice there's a skylight in the roof and a small extraction fan on the wall. It stares at me with its star shaped form and I try to find something else to focus on, but my eyes bounce around this shit hole and I'm forced to stare at the floor in an attempt to prevent my head spinning again. Composing myself, I turn to the door.

'You're going to have to do something, Chris,' I whisper to myself. 'What would James Bond do in this situation? I know! He'd break down the door!' Taking a step back, I brace myself against the wall. 'You can do it, buddy. One hard kick and the door will fly open.'

Releasing a high-pitched squeal, I leap into the air and karate kick the door. My right foot hits the lock, but instead of the door bursting open and handing me back my freedom, I find myself falling like a brick to the concrete floor. Scrambling to my feet, I contemplate karate kicking the door a second time, but instead I resort to banging on it as hard as possible with my fists and screaming my tits off. Pausing to listen for a response, I lean back against the wall and turn my attention to the skylight in the roof. Standing on tiptoe, I reach above my head and strain to seize hold of the catch. It's too high, so I decide to climb up onto the sink. Balancing precariously on the edge of the wash basin, I reach for the skylight and grab hold of the catch. Tugging at the metal handle it appears to be wedged shut. Taking a moment to adjust my balance, I take a firm grip on the catch and prepare to wrench it open. I pull down with all of my strength, but hearing a crack below, I lose my grip and leap off the edge of the sink as it breaks off the wall and crashes to the floor. Stumbling forward I skid in a puddle of urine and, slipping to my knees, I plunge my right hand into the brown, foul smelling toilet water. Hearing the door burst open on its hinges I glance over and see Si standing in the doorway with an amused look across his face.

At sunrise, we continue south on the M60 and skim past the cement town of Spassk-Dalny. A number of important battles had been fought here during the Russian Civil War between the White and Red Armies. To the east lies the Khanka Lake, one of the largest bodies of freshwater in Asia. With all of the windows down and the sunroof open, we merrily drive for 480km across the flat green countryside on the last leg of our journey. Morale is high, considering the potentially life threatening risk of poisoning ourselves with carbon monoxide. There is only the promise of Vladivostok at the end of this highway, a city that meant very little to us a couple of months ago but everything now. With each turn in the winding road we inch closer. It feels like a magnet is drawing us towards our ultimate destination, propelled by a momentum that is four weeks strong.

Looping around the Ussuri Bay, the traffic begins to build up and billboards begin to appear advertising Japanese cars for sale. Every man and his dog appear to be cashing in on the latest boom for importing cars from Japan. With butterflies in my stomach, we pass through a GAI checkpoint and begin to climb a steep gradient. Unless I'm completely mistaken, the Sierra appears to be running better now than it had before we left England. Si brakes sharply at the top of the hill and skids into a lay-by.

'Why have you stopped?' I smile.

'We're here.'

'What do you mean?'

'Look!'

Si points across the road at a crowd of people standing in front of a concrete monument. I'm rendered completely speechless when I see the striking sight of the 3D letters cast in iron, which spell "Vladivostok" in the Russian language. Si grabs his camera and takes a photograph of my ecstatic face next to the Sierra with the sign in the background. We have made it overland all the way from England to Vladivostok in our £300 Ford Sierra Sapphire. From Calais to Belgium, Germany to Eastern Europe, through the Baltic States into Russia, east over the Ural Mountains, across the notorious Zilov Gap and the entire length of Siberia all the way to Vladivostok on the Sea of Japan. Heading in the same direction with only one mission in mind, we have passed through nine time zones and driven a total distance of over 12,000km. Seeing these letters on top of this hill is undoubtedly the most amazing moment of my existence so far. We have come to the end of the road, quite literally. As the crow flies, Tokyo is only 659 miles away from Vladivostok, and the land border with North Korea is a relatively short drive south. We are now closer to the United States than Moscow! A complete sense of euphoria washes over me. It has all happened so fast. One minute we were deep in the wilderness and the next thing we know we have arrived at our ultimate destination. Part of me doesn't want our journey to end. I guess it will take some time for it to sink in. A bride rocks up wearing a huge white meringue of a wedding dress and stands with the groom in front of the Vladivostok sign. An enthusiastic photographer snaps away at their smiling faces, and a brass band begins to play under the trees. It almost feels like this whole event has been organised in honour of our arrival. Cashing in on the free entertainment, we dance around and hi-five each other with joy. People look at us strangely, and we laugh at the thought that they have absolutely no idea what we have just been through. I feel overwhelmed with emotion.

Buzzing with excitement, we accelerate over the brow of the hill and watch the city of Vladivostok slide dramatically into view. Singing 'The Final Countdown' by the rock band Europe, the road splits into a two-lane carriageway and we are sucked into a line of traffic that pushes us under a large concrete flyover and spits us out in the direction of Peter the Great Bay. Si battles against our fellow road users on the congested highway, and we speed towards the city centre and weave around trams and suicidal shoppers. Nudging around the main square, a monument dedicated to the Fighters for Soviet Power in the Far East looms above the traffic. In the historic area of the city we turn right at the impressive railway station, the terminating point of the Trans-Siberian, before following a steep coastal road around the Amursky Gulf. Si skids into a viewpoint overlooking the spectacular Zolotoy Rog Bay "The Golden Horn Bay" and the Sea of Japan.

'I can't believe we made it,' he smiles, perching himself on the hood of the car and inhaling the sea air. 'So, what happens now?'

I look out across the sparkling blue ocean. 'We could catch a ferry to Japan, drink shit loads of sake and watch sumo in Osaka.'

'To be honest with you, Chris, I'm feeling a little tired. Maybe we should chill out here for a while and then think about heading home.'

'Good idea,' I laugh. 'If we leave now we should be

home in time for tea in about five weeks.'

Glancing over my shoulder I notice a concrete hotel on the hill behind. 'Maybe we should treat ourselves nice and check into that hotel for the night. We have just driven halfway around the world.'

Si rubs his hands together. 'Sounds like a plan.'

We slide off the hood and drive swiftly to the gates of the Hotel Vladivostok. At the barrier to the private car park a guy hands me a ticket and we find an empty space close to the main doors. Entering a bustling lobby, we head straight for the reception desk and the smartly dressed woman checks us in with minimal fuss. The stocky guy standing next to me pays his bill with a large wad of cash that's stuffed into his back pocket. The room is a little pricey considering our slim line budget, but happy to push the boat out in celebration of our arrival, we agree to forget about money for one night and have some fun. The hotel room is clean and spacious and dumping our bags on the floor, we collapse onto our beds and are both asleep within seconds.

It's a Kind of Magic

I'm disturbed by the loud shrill of a telephone. I lift my head off the pillow and try to focus on my unfamiliar surroundings. The irritating ring tone begins to grate on my nerves, so I reach over and fumble for the receiver. Unable to find it, I grow increasingly agitated and accidentally knock over the lamp on the bedside table. It crashes to the floor. The phone continues to cry out for attention. Rolling onto my back, I swing my legs off the bed and pick up the phone.

'Hello?' I croak.

'Dobraye ootra, Mr Raven, this is reception.'

'Oh, hi, how's it going?' I smile at the cute voice on the end of the line.

'Sorry to disturb you, but it is nearly check out. Will you be staying another night?'

'Uh, yes, okay, we'd like to stay another night, please.'

'Spaceeba, Mr Raven. Sorry to have disturbed you.'

Shocked to discover we have slept for nearly eighteen hours straight, I drag myself into the shower. In a bid to snap myself out of my comatose state I blast myself with freezing cold water. I turn on the TV and watch CCTV, a Chinese news station, while I wait for Chris to get ready.

Wandering through the bustling streets of Vladivostok

in the early afternoon, we find ourselves down by the harbour. The city of Vladivostok loosely translates from Russian as "Ruler of the East", but it was known to the Chinese many centuries before by the less glorified name "Sea Cucumber Cliffs". Under Russian control, Vladivostok started life as a deserted military outpost at the end of the world, but it later grew into the largest Russian port on the Pacific Ocean and is home to the Russian Pacific Fleet. Weaving through the crowds of local day-trippers, holidaymakers and businessmen, who are gathered around brightly painted kiosks and beer tents, we head for a lively restaurant nestled beneath a green canopy. Chris suggests we treat ourselves to a juicy steak and gorging on red meat we watch a group of drunken youths sing around a portable karaoke machine. Reading from the guidebook, we're fascinated to learn that this region of the Far East experienced a mass influx of migrants from Ukraine in the early 20th Century. Lured by the promise of free land to raise cattle and grow wheat, they soon established a stable ethnic community in this region of Russia in a territory that became known as the Zeleny Klyn "Green Ukraine". First arriving by ship from Odessa to Vladivostok in April 1883, the population of Ukrainian migrants increased to 310,000 by 1897, with a further 78,000 arriving here in 1907. Ethnic Koreans once inhabited this region of Russia around Vladivostok, but during Stalinist rule over 200,000 were deported to Uzbekistan and Kazakhstan between 1937 and 1939. Approximately 100,000 Koreans tragically died during transportation in cattle trains as a result of starvation, illness and freezing conditions.

We continue our celebratory stroll along the harbour and the Golden Horn Bay, that's separated by cliffs from the Peter the Great Gulf. In the summer of 1859, Governor-

General of Eastern Siberia, Nikolay N. Muravyov, visited this peninsula and thought how similar it was to the Bay of the Golden Horn in Istanbul. Making a circuit around the city, we pass rows of Chinese restaurants and stumble across the newly renovated Nikolai's Triumphal Arch (Arch of Prince Nicholas), first built in 1891. The grand reopening of the renovated arch took place only three weeks ago, on the 135th anniversary of Nicholas's birth and the 85th anniversary of the tragic death of the last Russian tsar and his family in Yekaterinburg. It has been lovingly restored almost in its original appearance with two-thirds original works of the sculptors, painters and ceramists.

In need of a well-earned drink we return to the hotel and follow signs to a small bar in the basement. Chris orders a whiskey and I settle for vodka on the rocks. We sip the drinks and fall into conversation with the waitress who we learn is called Anika. She's six feet tall and has the longest legs I have ever seen. She sits beside me, her short black skirt clinging to the tops of her thighs. Chris tells the story about how we have driven all the way to Vladivostok from the UK. Anika laughs and changes the subject, but Chris perseveres and continues to share details of our great adventure. Suddenly, an enormous guy wearing a purple tracksuit enters the bar. He overhears our conversation and confidently joins our table. We discover that Yegor is an ex-Olympic Russian heavyweight boxing champion, who lived in Beverly Hills for ten years in a mansion next door to the 1980s American pop star MC Hammer. Much to our surprise, he seems genuinely fascinated by our road trip.

'I welcome you to Vladivostok,' he bellows, raising his glass.

We both raise our drinks.

'Nastrovia,' Chris sings.

Anika appears to be star struck and immediately fixes us all new drinks. Yegor is the strongest guy I have ever met. His hands are the size of Chris's head and his neck is as thick as a tree trunk. With spiky blonde hair and a ridiculously square jaw, he looks uncannily like Dolph Lundgren, the actor who played the Russian boxer in the 1985 movie classic 'Rocky IV'. He impresses us with the story of how he had to quit boxing after he was shot in the stomach. He lifts up his t-shirt and shows us the scar. We gasp in amazement at hearing how he once worked as a bodyguard for a rich businessman and had taken a bullet for him. He hasn't been able to box professionally since. The guy's enthusiasm and energy is impressive. He seems as soft as a pussycat, and I can only imagine that it's the knowledge of his strength and abilities, which allow him to behave so passively. He doesn't need to put up a front, or prove that he is stronger or more capable. It's just an unspoken fact, an inner confidence that naturally demands respect. We look tiny sat next to this giant and we're surprised when he challenges us to an arm wrestle. The guy swiftly offers Chris his index finger and, with slight hesitation, Chris wraps the palm of his hand around his enormous digit. Yegor beats him with incredible ease and I sit back in awe of this guy's outrageous strength. I nip to the toilet and pass six Japanese guys exiting the hotel sauna. They're all wearing matching yellow swimming trunks and they chatter and laugh loudly with their bottles of Asahi beer. Swaying at the urinal, I catch myself humming 'Hammer Time' and I chuckle in amusement when I remember why. I up-tempo and dance Hammer-style over to the sink. Exiting the toilet I hear the Japanese guy's singing karaoke in a nearby room. I take a peek through a gap in the door and smile when I see them listening to one of the guys belting out a sentimental love song into a microphone. Anika enters the corridor and catwalks towards me with a tray full of Asahi beer.

'Oh, hi,' I grin.

'You like karaoke, Simon?'

'No, I mean, yes, it's great.'

'Do you want to use machine?'

'Maybe later,' I reply feeling immediately embarrassed.

'Okay, if you need anything you only have to ask.'

Anika looks deep into my eyes before disappearing into the room. I return to the bar. Chris immediately introduces me to Seung, a bizarre looking chap in his late twenties from Seoul, who has a round, pale face and dark rings under his eyes. Wearing thick brown framed glasses and sporting a sharp bowl cut, he's quick to inform me that he's paralyzed down the left side of his face. I learn that his affliction is stress related. He appears to be deeply depressed, and he confides in me that he has lost a lot of confidence as a result of his condition, especially with women.

'Girls like a guy who can smile,' he sighs, '…and I can't smile.'

Seung explains that society in South Korea is incredibly competitive, and that many people suffer from stress related illness. He seems fascinated by our travels, and shows great admiration for tossing aside our careers and heading off on an adventure into the unknown. It is something he admits he could never imagine doing. In his society the measure of success is directly related to material wealth and the achievements in your career. His family would be ashamed of him if he were to turn his back on the family business and disappear on a whim.

Chris nudges me with his elbow. 'Hey, Yegor knows someone who might be interested in buying the Sierra.'

'Really?'

Yegor nods. 'Yes, my friend Artur is croupier in hotel casino. He has many connections. He buy car from you.'

Seeing Anika return to the bar, she throws me a testicle-tingling gaze and starts chatting to the older woman, who is vigorously crushing ice.

'We go!' Yegor commands downing his vodka.

'Where?' I frown, disappointed by the idea of a sudden departure.

'To meet Artur,' Chris grins, slamming his drink on the table.

'I'm going to chill out here with Seung for a bit. You go.'

Chris looks surprised by my lack of enthusiasm.

Yegor looks over at Anika and then throws me a wink. 'I wish you luck,' he smiles.

Seung half yawns and heads off to bed. I sit on my own and watch the bar slowly empty. The Japanese guys finish singing karaoke and make their way to the casino, and the older woman working behind the bar kisses her colleague goodnight and heads off home. As I'd hoped, Anika seems keen for me to stick around.

'Simon, do you believe in magic?'

'Magic?'

'Da, magic,' she smiles, sitting down beside me.

'I'm not sure.'

'Why not sure? I believe in magic.'

'What kind of magic do you believe in?'

'Good magic. I like to read books about...how you say...fantasy?'

'Oh, you mean stories about witches and wizards, that kind of thing?'

'Da.'

'I haven't read anything like that for years.'

'Close your eyes.'

'Why?' I laugh nervously.

'I want to show you magic.'

Reluctantly, I do as she asks and feeling her soft fingertips against my temple I smile at the sensation of the intimacy and silence. I relax and begin to feel a warm energy flowing into my body through her fingers. It trickles past my ears and spreads across my shoulders and down my spine.

'Can you feel it?' she whispers, breaking the silence.

'Yes, I think I can.'

'It is magic, Simon.'

The warm sensation fills my entire body, reaching all the way down to the tips of my toes. I shift in my seat and clear my throat. Anika drops her hands and sits back as the warm energy continues to circulate around my body.

* * *

What the hell am I doing? I'm in an elevator with an ex-Olympic boxer, who definitely has connections with the Russian Mafia and an index finger that could break my spine. The journey seems to be taking forever; it's the slowest elevator in the world. Yegor looks down at me, and smiles. I crank my neck and smile back. Come on! How long does it take to travel up seven floors? I know Yegor must weigh roughly the same as a Blue Whale, but this is ridiculous. The silence is killing me. I have to say something.

'So, did it hurt when you got shot?' I beam.

Yegor furrows his brow and I cringe with embarrassment. Thankfully, the elevator doors slide open before he has time to answer. We walk towards a room at the far end of the corridor. Yegor invites me into a large penthouse suite, with an impressive view of the bay. He leads me through to the lounge, where a smartly dressed guy and an attractive woman sit slouched on a corner sofa. I immediately notice two lines of cocaine on the glass coffee table in front of them. Yegor introduces me to Artur and Katya. Artur works in the hotel casino and I think Katya is possibly a lady of the night. Here in Russia sleeping with a prostitute appears to be as normal as brushing your teeth; although, I could be wrong, she could be Artur's girlfriend. Artur shakes my hand before using a thin silver pipe to snort one of the lines of cocaine up his left nostril. He throws his head back and hands Katya the pipe. She leans forward and clears the second line in a swift motion. They both sniff hard and simultaneously grab their drinks off the coffee table.

'Please, take a seat,' Yegor smiles.

Artur immediately begins lining up more cocaine with a credit card.

'You would like?' he asks.

No thanks,' I smile.

Katya looks over at me, and sniffs. She stares deep into my eyes.

'Chris, you want vodka?' Yegor shouts across the room.

'That would be great, spaceeba.'

Yegor pours the drink and places it in front of me. 'Drink and be merry,' he laughs.

Yegor sits down on the sofa beside Artur and talks to him in Russian. Artur listens carefully and nods his head. They both lean back and sip their drinks.

'Chris, I tell Artur about your car.'

'Yeah, it's a Ford Sierra Sapphire.'

'Maybe I interested,' Artur smiles.

'Really?'

'Da, how much you sell?'

I shrug my shoulders. 'I don't know. We've driven it a long way, so it needs a few repairs.'

'The car is old?'

'It rolled off the production line in nineteen eighty-nine.'

'That's old,' he smiles, turning to Yegor. 'It has big engine?'

'About that big,' I reply, holding my hands roughly three feet apart.

Artur bursts out laughing. 'You funny man, Chris.'

Knocking back a second glass of vodka, I find myself jabbering away like I'm with old friends. Yegor makes a call and moments later two beautiful women enter the room. Yegor immediately disappears into the bedroom with one of the girls. Katya flicks on MTV and blasts up the volume.

'So, Chris, now you in Vladivostok what you do?' Artur grins.

'Well, I only have a small amount of money left. I need to return home soon.'

'Where is home?'

'Daventry.'

Artur frowns. 'Dovintery?'

'No, Daventry. It's in England.'

'Ah, David Beckham,' he smiles.

'You like David Beckham?'

'Da, he has cool hair.' Artur looks suddenly embarrassed by what he has just said and darts paranoid glances around the room. 'Why you not drive home to Dovintery?' He asks with wide eyes.

'No way, it's too far. I don't think my body would be able to withstand the pain. We thought about catching the ferry to Japan and flying home from there, but our money situation is a problem.'

'Get Trans-Siberian train to Moscow,' Artur suggests.

'I was thinking about that.'

Artur clicks his fingers. 'You go to China!'

'But we don't have a visa.'

'No problem, Chris, there is Chinese Consulate in Khabarovsk. You are very close. You should go.'

'That's actually not a bad idea! Hey, Artur, you still want my car?'

'Da, I still interested, but how much for car?'

'I don't want your money. I will give it to you for free.'

Artur looks confused. 'No money?'

'Yes, no money.'

'You joke with me, Chris.'

'I'm serious. I want you to have the car.'

'Spaceeba,' he laughs, shaking my hand vigorously.

I jab around inside my pockets for the keys, but I remember I've left them in the room.

'I want to give you the keys,' I sing, shifting around on the sofa.

Artur frowns. 'Keys for car?'

'Yes, the keys! I want to give you the keys to the car!'

Artur nods vigorously, and sniffs. 'Okay, I will take your keys.'

Leaping to my feet, I march across the hotel room like a soldier on parade. Artur charges after me and meets me at the door.

'Where you go?'

'I go to my room…to get the keys for the car.'

'But what about girls?' he whispers, pointing over his shoulder.

I see Katya dancing in front of the TV with the girl in thigh length boots. They blow me a kiss.

'What's your room number?' he grins.

'Three three two, I'll be right back.'

Charging out of the room, I make my way speedily down the corridor. Picking up pace, I decide to take the stairs and jump two to three steps at a time. I arrive at my room and leap inside. I zip around the beds faster than Speedy Gonzalez and snatch the car keys off the bedside table. Just as I'm about to leave I hear a knock at the door. I peer through the spy hole and see Katya standing outside the room with the girl wearing thigh length boots.

Foot People

With clothes spilling out of our rucksacks, we stumble into the reception area and look around for Artur. He's nowhere to be seen.

'Where is he?' Si grumbles.

'If he's got any sense he'll still be in bed.'

'I can't believe you gave him the Sierra. You could have asked me first. We could've sold it for some cash.'

'Have you seen the state of it? You wouldn't be able to sell that old rust bucket even if it was the last car on the planet. Artur is a cool guy. He's practically doing us a favour taking it off our hands.'

Si reluctantly agrees.

'Tell you what, why don't you go and check us out of the hotel while I wait here for Artur?'

Si nods and trudges over to the reception desk. Artur slides up beside me, his eyes are bloodshot and his bright blue shirt is buttoned up the wrong holes.

'Sorry I late,' he pants, darting glances around the foyer.

'No problem, we've only just got here.'

'You give me car, no money?'

'Of course, I have the keys.'

'Drive to top of hill behind hotel. I meet you in five

minutes. My boss no see, da?'

'No problem'

We dump our rucksacks on the backseat and drive the battered Sierra to the top of the hill behind the hotel. It feels strange to be behind the wheel again, and it puzzles me how we managed to live for so long in such appalling conditions. When we were on the road it felt normal, we were in the same state as the Sierra, all filthy and clapped out, and I realise now how close we were to failing in our mission. The interior is completely covered in dust and the floor is littered with food wrappers and empty water bottles. It smells disgusting, and the thought of having to sleep in here makes me feel physically sick. How we did it I'll never know. Adrenaline, determination and complete insanity can be the only answer. On the passenger window I scribble "UK to Vladivostok 2003" in the dirt. Even though the whole exhaust system is hanging off and all four tyres are threadbare, Artur is one lucky guy. For a start, there aren't any Ford Sierra's in Vladivostok, as far as we know, so when it's fixed he'll be driving around in one of the coolest cars in the city. Well, maybe not the coolest car, but certainly one of the most original. Artur meets us on the hill and his eyes light up when he sees the Sierra. He loves the car and dances around it. I take a photo of Artur holding up the car keys.

'Russia and England, friends!' he cries.

He looks so happy. We show him the customs declaration form, and he puts our minds at rest by informing us that his girlfriend's father is a traffic officer and that anything can be arranged in Russia if you know the right people. We're a little reluctant to give him the vehicle documents, but he insists that it is necessary in order to register the car as a Russian vehicle. It's time for us to depart and say farewell to our trusty time machine.

Artur leaps into the car without even flinching at the smell and strikes the engine. I remember I've left something in the glove box and grab the SAS Survival Guide and the road atlas. They may come in handy for another adventure. Fighting back the tears, we watch our beloved Sierra disappear and splutter out of sight in a cloud of black smoke.

'I can't believe it's over,' I sigh, swinging my rucksack over my shoulder.

Si nods. 'Yep, it looks like we're back to being just simple foot people.'

We both smile and glance out across the ocean.

We're about to make the journey down to the railway station, when I notice a vehicle making its way up the winding road. It's the Germans! Their unmistakable bright orange truck skids into the hotel car park. They leap out and swing each other around in celebration of their arrival. We consider going down to congratulate them, but decide to let them enjoy their moment. They've come a long way. They deserve it.

Feeling strangely vulnerable without the safety of the Sierra, like a tortoise without its shell, I follow Si through the busy city streets and we enter the chaos of the train station. Looking up at the departure board we're unable to see Khabarovsk, so we weave down the stairs and join a long queue at the ticket counter. As we inch forward, a guy wearing military uniform pushes to the front of the queue. The people standing behind mutter under their breath. We eventually make it to the window and I smile at the woman sat behind the glass.

'Khabarovsk?' I smile.

'Da,' she nods.

'Dva, spaceeba,' I reply, raising two fingers.

She circles the price on the ticket with a green pen and

slides it beneath the window. The train leaves at 20.45. With four hours to kill, we chill out in a small café inside the station and write up our notes. It's busy with travellers heading west across this huge country. A businessman whips back a shot of vodka at the counter. The clock strikes seven, so we have a look around the station and admire this magnificent historic building. The train station's pride is its roof, which is decorated with metallic coping and small figured gable windows, and the walls are covered with mosaics depicting horsemen, fairy birds, berries and fruits. Si points out an old steam locomotive on the platform. The number 9288 is inscribed on the stela and identifies the distance between Moscow and Vladivostok in kilometres. In 1891, the construction of the Trans-Siberian Railroad began right here in this very city. Anxious to find our train, we head for the platform and identify the correct carriage. The Khabarovsk-Vladivostok express train is surprisingly quiet, which is great because we have the whole cabin to ourselves. The train pulls out of the station and we stare out of the window. The forest landscape and the small rural communities flash by at speed, and I smile at the thought that we know what it's really like out there in the depths of the Siberian wilderness. We call it a night after a bite to eat in the buffet car, and collapsing onto my bunk I fall asleep to the awesome sound of the clattering carriages.

* * *

The door to our compartment slams open and a deep voice shouts "Khabarovsk!" We quickly gather together our belongings and shuffle off the train. Chris stands motionless on the platform and looks incredibly dazed. Hoards of people make their way towards the exit, knocking us to one side as they rush by. It's six o'clock in the morning, and even though I had a good nights sleep my eyes refuse to open. I sit on my rucksack and fish my contact lens case out of my pocket. Balancing the white plastic container on my knee, I manage to rinse out each lens with solution before forcing them into my eyes. Chris grabs a bottle of warm water out of his bag and pours half of it down his throat and the other half over his greasy face. We make our way out of the railway station and grab a taxi to the Hotel Intourist, which is close to the Chinese Consulate. Entering the plush hotel, we make our way over to the information counter and wait patiently for the woman to finish speaking on the phone. She lowers the receiver and looks over.

'Dobry den,' Chris smiles. 'Do you speak English?'

'A little,' she replies. 'How can I help you?'

'We'd like to go to China, please.'

She looks puzzled. 'China?'

'Yes.'

'You must travel by boat,' the woman sighs.

'Can we arrange this here?'

'I must ask, please wait.'

The girl makes a call and within seconds of placing down the receiver a smartly dressed middle-aged woman, with bleached blonde hair and bright red lipstick, marches towards us across the hotel lobby.

'Good morning,' she smiles, reaching out her hand. 'My name is Ksenia. Where are you from?'

'We're from England,' I reply.

She looks excited. 'You are the first English people I have met. I thought you were Italian. What are you doing here in Khabarovsk?'

'We've just driven from England to Vladivostok,' Chris beams, straightening his posture.

Ksenia looks incredibly surprised. 'You have driven from England to Vladivostok? Oh, fantastic, that is a big distance. Congratulations.'

'Finally, someone believes us,' Chris smiles.

'Yes, I believe you. My teacher of English lived in London for ten years. She was married to a businessman from Croydon. He too liked to drive. They travelled to Spain by car. I am sorry if my English is not good.'

'Your English is excellent,' I reply.

'Thank you, but I still have much to learn. Please allow me to welcome you both to Khabarovsk. My colleague tells me you would like to go to the Chinese border town of Fuyuan on a day trip?'

Chris frowns. 'Not a day trip. We want to travel into China.'

'You do not return to Russia?'

'No, we want a one way boat to the border.'

'So you are not aware the border with China has been closed for six months?'

I cast Chris a look of concern. 'We had no idea.'

'We are waiting to find out if it will reopen. We have a Russian group who would like to visit the market tomorrow.'

'Why has it been closed?' Chris asks.

'Have you heard of SARS? There was a small outbreak in southern China. The government in Moscow decided to close the border to prevent the spread of the virsus into Russia. It has been very bad for business. Your arrangement is not a common request, so I must make a few telephone calls. Please wait here for a moment.'

Ksenia disappears into her office. We pace around the reception area and wait over half-an-hour for her to return. I begin to wonder if it might not be possible to travel to China after all. She finally emerges from her office and marches across the hotel lobby clutching a piece of paper.

'I can arrange everything for you,' she nods, a little out of breath, 'including the boat to Fuyuan and a bus transfer to Harbin, but it will cost sixty US dollars each. I will be honest with you. We must bribe the officials to let you cross the border. My contact in China seems to think it will be possible, but there is a risk they may refuse you entry. As far as I know, you are the first foreign tourists to cross this border into China since the nineteen nineties. It was a Ukrainian man who came here. He never returned, so I assume he managed to enter China on the other side without a problem. You have been fortunate the border has reopened again after six months. Maybe you have luck on your side. Nothing is guaranteed, but you will be part of a tour group so I think it will be okay.'

'Thanks for all of your help, Ksenia, 'I smile, relieved by the good news. 'We had no idea it was going to be such a problem.'

'Most people who cross this border are Russians buying electrical goods from the market in Fuyuan to sell here in Khabarovsk.

'What about visas?'

'You can get a tourist visa from the Chinese Consulate today,' she replies, glancing down at her watch. 'Are you staying at this hotel?'

'Yes, I guess so. We haven't sorted anything out yet.'

'I will have your tickets ready for you by this afternoon, so please arrange your visas now and I will give you all of the information you need when you return from the consulate.'

Checking in at reception, we grit our teeth and pay US$100 for a double room. Exiting the hotel, we follow a path that leads around the back of the building and down a flight of stone steps. We cross a pleasant tree lined park that runs alongside the Amur River and pass the impressive Lenin Stadium, with its large statues of a boxer and an ice skater outside the gates. The next building along is the Chinese Consulate. Grabbing a ticket, we join a long queue outside and wait patiently in the sunshine. It takes over three hours and a further US$60 to get a one month visa glued into our passports. Heading back to the hotel via the banks of the Amur River, Ksenia presents us with our tickets for the boat. She informs us that the hydrofoil departs tomorrow morning at 7am. All the necessary arrangements have been made, and a Chinese tour operator called Yut will meet us on the other side. Feeling completely exhausted and utterly relieved to have sorted everything out, we thank her and crash out in the hotel room. I lie paralysed on my bed and stare up at the ceiling. The night sweats take hold of my body and I'm tormented by a feverish sleep. Images from our journey flash in front of my eyes and I struggle to remember where we are. I replay the scene over in my mind of the horrific car accident we saw while crossing the Ural Mountains, and I see the ghostly figure of the dead driver lying stretched out in the road. Gliding through the remote Siberian villages locked in time, I see children chasing rusty metal hoops and a girl dressed in a pink party frock on a swing hung from the branches of a tree. Chimneys bellow black smoke into the air, as we swoop over the concrete city suburbs. Flames reach out from forest fires and I can feel the immense heat on my skin. My mind races and we're driving along a dusty potholed track. We pass hunched figures, who turn for a brief second; their faces like masks, carved from dark wood.

A Touch of SARS

I'm startled by the beeping sound of my alarm clock. I look over at Si, who is sat on the edge of his bed with his head in his hands. Too tired to speak, we slowly get dressed in silence and make our way down to reception. My rucksack feels unnaturally heavy and I begin to suspect someone may have removed my clothes during the night and replaced them with rocks. We're met by Ksenia outside the elevator.

'Good morning!' she sings from behind a pair of enormous sunglasses. 'Your transport to the boat terminal is waiting outside. Please follow me.'

We clamber into the back of an awaiting taxi, and Ksenia wishes us luck on our journey before waving the clumsy foreigners farewell. Within no time at all we arrive at the boat terminal. Si quickly grabs some water and a sack of potato chips from a small kiosk, before we are escorted to a small brick building where we join a long queue of people at passport control. Reaching the front of the queue, we hand over our documents to the Russian official sat behind the desk. A spotlight glares in my face, and I'm ordered to stand behind a yellow line with my hands by my sides. I suddenly remember the Sierra. Technically speaking, we're not supposed to be leaving

Russia from this exit point and without the car. The border crossing with Narva in Estonia is where we're officially supposed to exit the country. I try to stay relaxed, which is challenging with a bright light shinning in my eyes and a scary customs official interrogating my every move. Thankfully, he doesn't mention the Sierra and handing back my passport he waves me through. Si also makes it through smoothly, and we're greeted at the hydrofoil by two female customs officials dressed in military uniform. Wearing black leather boots, both women are blonde and extremely attractive. They check our exit stamps and dismiss us without a smile. We find our way onto the boat and sit at a table opposite two women and a teenage kid who looks sulkily out of the window. I can hear his thoughts, "I hate you! I didn't ask to be born. Why can't you all just leave me alone?" The woman sat next to the grumpy teenager opens a plastic container filled with sandwiches and places them in the centre of the table. She offers us both one, and we gratefully devour a ham sandwich loaded with pickled gherkins. Si tears open the sack of potato chips in a gesture of good will, and we all munch happily in silence as the boat pulls away from the pier. The hydrofoil rockets down the Amur River, which is known to the Chinese as the Heilong Jiang "Black Dragon". The Kaluga fish that inhabit these waters can grow to a whopping 5.6 metres. I peer out across the river, and look for signs of the Amur highway that had transported us to Vladivostok. Si fishes a pocket atlas out of his rucksack and we study the huge landmass of China. We have yet to purchase a guidebook, and we begin to wonder how we'll find our way from the city of Harbin in the north to Kunming in the south; which is a staggering 3,900km away.

Two hours pass and I'm awoken by the sound of the

hydrofoils powerful engines cutting out. As the boat drifts to a halt, two Chinese customs officials wearing green uniforms climb aboard. I'm surprised to see they are both wearing white surgical masks and one of the women is carrying what appears to be some kind of scan gun. She methodically works her way from one end of the boat to the other, and fires a red beam of light at a chubby lady a few seats away. The Russian woman looks stunned as the laser bounces off her wrinkled forehead. They appear to be checking people's body temperature in a bid to prevent the spread of SARS. I begin to feel hot and sweaty and pray my body temperature isn't artificially higher than it should normally be. Images flash through my mind of being carried off the boat and quarantined inside an oxygen bubble for years in some remote hospital in the Heilongjiang Province of northern China. The official approaches me and raises the gun to my forehead. I look into her brown eyes and brace myself. She pulls the trigger and hearing a healthy sounding beep I breathe out a sigh of relief. She then points it at Si, who also looks rather flustered, but it beeps and she continues down the boat. We plant our feet firmly on Chinese soil and a huge crimson flag flaps vigorously in the warm breeze. A smartly dressed Chinese woman with a short boyish haircut approaches us. It's Yut. She welcomes us both to China and appears intrigued to meet two guys from England. She doesn't speak English and giggles every time we say something. Yut personally escorts us through customs, and we're greatly surprised by the welcoming reception we receive from the Chinese officials. They quickly stamp our passports, and we're made to feel like VIP's as we're led to an awaiting mini bus outside. We're transported a few miles down the road to a busy market. It's absolute mayhem, with hoards of local Chinese shoppers and market traders filling every inch of the street. The Russian day-trippers collapse out of the mini bus, and disperse into the crowds to purchase cheap TV's, stereos, satellite dishes and portable karaoke machines. Within seconds, we find ourselves hurtling along the main street of Fuyuan. The town looks fairly modern and newly constructed buildings stand either side of a tarmac road. Large white Chinese characters printed on red silky banners hang across the front of the buildings along the main street, and splashes of gold paint decorate the roofs, giving the place an air of tackiness. We pull up outside a large building, which I presume is the bus station. Yut races inside and pays in cash for two tickets to Harbin, China's northern city. We then rush out of the bus station and follow her to a beat-up sleeper coach. A luggage handler immediately tears our rucksacks off our shoulders and adds them to the cargo that's piled up on the ground. Bowing her head, Yut says something to us in Chinese before dashing off back to her Russian tour group. We suddenly feel incredibly vulnerable in this completely alien world. The many people standing around the bus stare at us with intrigue and two guys sitting on a wall laugh at our big feet. It's impossible to blend in here. At least in Russia if we kept our mouth's shut we could have been mistaken for being locals, but here it's glaringly obvious we're not from around these parts. A brown sack begins to move by itself and I hear yapping coming from inside. I realise it's a bag of puppies, most probably on route to the nearest town of Jiamusi or to a Harbin restaurant.

Our fellow passengers eventually start to board the bus, so we follow their lead. It's incredibly cramped inside and the putrid smell of sweaty feet hits me hard, as we squeeze down the narrow aisle. Si contorts his body into his cot close to the window, and a curious Chinese guy sat nearby stares up at me as I slip off my trainers and haul myself over his head. The bunks are less than one and a half metres long, making it physically impossible to stretch out our legs. I console myself with the thought that at least it's only a fifteen hour journey. The driver of the bus stands outside and chats to a guy on a moped. He seems quite oblivious to the fact that his bus is ready to depart and everyone on board is raring to go. Eventually, the driver rocks this dirty bus out of town and into the barren countryside of northern China. The driver switches on the onboard entertainment system and blasts Chinese music from the stereo. Si's head is literally three inches away from the speaker embedded in the ceiling, and I try not to laugh when we're flung from side to side on the bumpy road to Harbin. Passing through small towns, we watch dogs scavenging for food and I study the hard faces of people who live in a corner of the world I hardly knew existed. Featherless chickens scratch and peck at the dry earth, while toothless hags thrust unrecognisable fried cuisine through the bus windows. Hardened by our journey across Siberia, we lie back and embrace the unknown. In a world where anything can and will happen, fear for us has finally left the building, and when and where our journey will come to an end it seems clear now is a question we have always faced.

Back to Bateman

'Right now guys settle down,' yells Bateman, the nightshift supervisor. 'It's another busy night tonight. We've got ninety-five thousand to pick, so I want you all to pull your fingers out of your backsides and get stacking those boxes.'

The time is 6:58pm. It's getting dark outside and I'm sitting in a canteen with Chris surrounded by a hundred exhausted fellow freezer workers. We're all dressed like we're about to ski down Mont Blanc, and are minutes away from throwing ourselves once more into a 12-hour nightshift in the harsh conditions of the -30°C freezer.

'What are you still doing here?' Bateman yells. 'There's work to be done. Come on, move!'

A loud groan fills the canteen.

We're back in the freezer and back to Bateman. Even though it's only been fourteen days since our jumbo touched down on UK soil, our road trip to Vladivostok feels like a distant memory. Our travels in China had been incredible. From the industrial city of Harbin we caught a train to Beijing, the Mecca of the People's Republic of China, where we continued directly south to Zhengzhou to visit the Shaolin temple and the 10,000 students who train Kung Fu. Onwards to Xian, to see the awe-inspiring

Terracotta Warriors, to Chengdu to play with the baby pandas, before travelling south to Kunming to cross the border into the South East Asian country of Laos. Reaching Bangkok in Thailand, "land of smiles", we explored one of the craziest cities in the world, with its fast-paced sticky street life, amazing temples and disturbing ping-pong shows. Arriving on the paradise island of Koh Phangan, we spent the last few weeks of our journey swimming in the beautiful blue ocean, eating fresh fish, swinging in hammocks and drinking buckets of Thai whiskey. We had certainly ended our trip in style. With tanned faces we made our way back to Bangkok, where we purchased a one way ticket to Heathrow via Kuwait City for £195. Baghdad was heavily bombed only six months ago, so it was crazy to fly over the Middle East and see enormous oil fields and American soldiers wearing desert combat uniforms. Much to our relief, we made it back to old Blighty "God save the Queen" without being blown out of the sky by a rocket launcher. Catching a National Express coach to our hometown of Daventry, we walked the last mile to our house where our journey had first begun. With dirty rucksacks over our shoulders, we felt like men returning home from war, well, not quite, but it felt pretty good all the same. I wanted to shout out to everyone walking down the street "we've just driven to Vladivostok in a £300 Ford Sierra", but of course I didn't. Our family was in the kitchen when we arrived at the house. It was a lovely surprise.

Standing by a busy chute rammed with heavy boxes of frozen oven chips, I physically and mentally prepare myself for the long cold night ahead. Glancing around, I notice nothing has changed it's all exactly the same. The Kurdish guys and Lefty seem really pleased to see us again.

Chris slides up to me with a broom in his hand. 'I'm chasing frozen peas for a living.'

I burst out laughing. 'I thought the boss only gave that job to complete idiots.'

'I can't believe we're back in this ice box,' he sighs. 'We need to go on another adventure, and sharpish.'

We turn and see Bateman marching towards us. '...Ravens! It's a busy night tonight. Why aren't you working?'

'We are working,' Chris snaps, his face bursting with frustration.

'Do I look like I was born yesterday?'

Chris shakes his head. 'Uh, nope, you sure don't.''

'Look, I know your game. One more strike and you're both out. Kapish?'

I see Lefty tiptoe up behind Bateman. He whips his Aston Villa bobble hat off his head. We both look in surprise, as a mass of curly black hair flops down either side of his fat face. Bateman looks embarrassed and turns red. The whole hard man image immediately disappears. Furious, he chases after Lefty between the chutes.

A voice calls over. 'Excuse me, please. You help?'

We turn and see a guy cradling a box of frozen vegetables in his arms. 'You tell me, please, if vegetables go in cage four or six?'

'Cage six is for frozen bread and cage four is for meat. Vegetables go in cage three,' I shout back over the noise of a nearby hydraulic machine.

'Thank you,' the guy smiles.

'Hey, where are you from?'

'I am from Sao Paulo in Brazil,' he replies.

Chris turns to me, and winks. 'Brazil!'

Carnival Express
SIMON RAVEN   CHRIS RAVEN

A South America Adventure

From bull's testicles in Buenos Aires to bums and boobs on the beaches of Brazil, Simon and Chris embark on a new adventure as they attempt to traverse the Trans-oceanic highway by express bus from the Pacific to the Atlantic Coast of South America. Not always getting it right, the hapless heroes tango through the Argentinean vineyards, cycle to the Moon in the Atacama Desert, survive death roads in the Peruvian Andes and venture deep into the heart of the Amazon jungle with only one mission in mind – to go in search of the real carnival!

'Carnival Express' is the third book in the 'Ravens on the Road' travel trilogy.

Black Sea Circuit
SIMON RAVEN   CHRIS RAVEN

An Adventure Through the Caucasus

The legends of Jason and the Argonauts, Noah's Ark and a tribe of fierce female warriors known as the Amazons all originate from the Black Sea. Gripped by curiosity, Simon and Chris fire up their twenty year old Volvo that looks, "as rustic and weather-beaten as a Cold War tank" and embark on a quest to drive full circle around this ancient body of water at the birthplace of civilisation.

In the shadow of rising tension in Ukraine, the brothers get up close and personal with the fascinating people who inhabit the six nations that surround these colourful shores. Living on the road like the nomadic horse bowmen who once ruled the steppe grasslands, they explore Crimea, the Caucasus region of southern Russia's "Wild West", the Georgian kingdom of Colchis, Turkey's Pontic coast, the megacity of Istanbul and complete their journey in Romania at the outfall of the mighty River Danube.

A career in overland adventure travel was launched when Simon and Chris coaxed a rusty Ford Sierra across Siberia from the UK to Vladivostok. Priding themselves in going it alone, the brothers have been noted by Lonely Planet for their talent to portray an "accurate view of what to expect".

Living the Linger
SIMON RAVEN   CHRIS RAVEN

Bumbling Through Backcountry USA

Disillusioned with life in the big city, two brothers embark on a road trip from Seattle to Los Angeles through backcountry USA.

The sudden break up with girlfriend Emily Willow finds Simon Raven, ex-amateur rock God and bored internet producer, on a Boeing 747 bound for Seattle. Led by his twin brother, Chris, who is more than happy to exchange a career in fashion photography for the open road, they embark on a buttock-clenching journey of paranoia and self-doubt, as they traverse Interstate Highway 15 through backcountry America.

Along the way the hapless heroes bumble through bear infested wilderness, meet the eccentric and plain weird on the American freeway, escape a bullwhip wielding maniac in Montana and survive the evils of Las Vegas. Testing their friendship to the limit as they battle to reach their nirvana, which exists in the form of the bikini beaches of California, the brothers find inspiration on a journey that exposes the stark truth about work and relationships and which asks the question - what do you really want to do with your life?

'Living the Linger' is the first book in the 'Ravens on the Road' travel trilogy.

Printed in Great Britain
by Amazon